AF574673

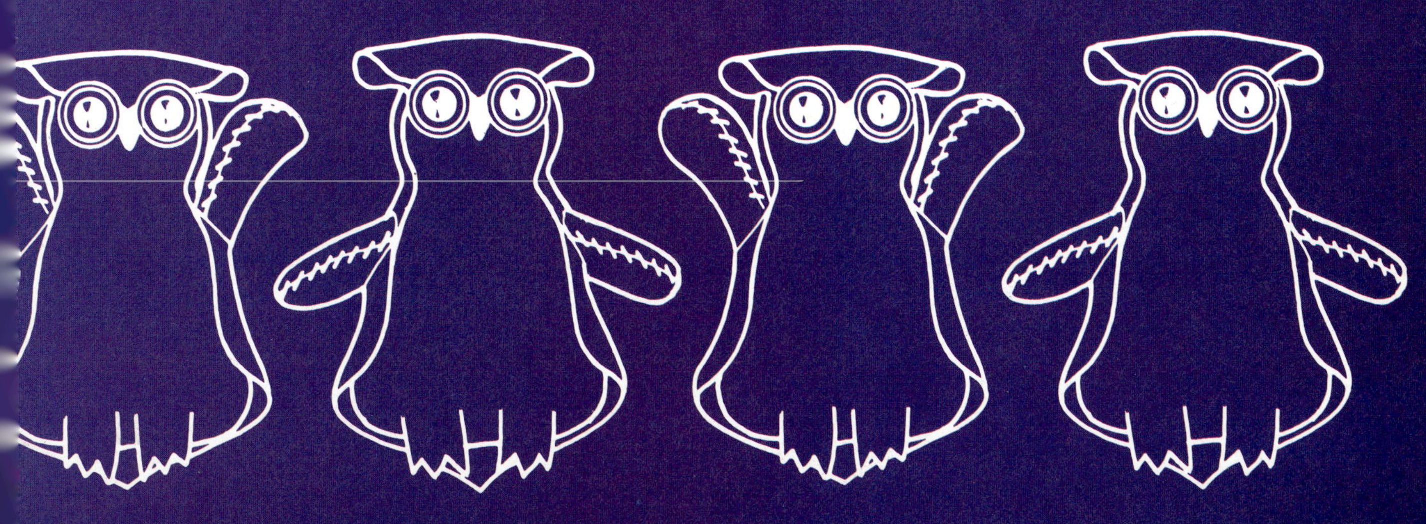

SOFT TOYS TO MAKE FOR CHILDREN

Golden Hands Books

Marshall Cavendish
London and New York

Edited by Alison Louw

Published by Marshall Cavendish Publications Limited,
58 Old Compton Street,
London W1V 5PA

This material was first published
by Marshall Cavendish Limited
in *The Golden Hands Toy Box.*

This volume first published 1975

Printed in Great Britain by Severn Valley Press Limited.

ISBN 0 85685 144 2

introduction

Every mother is familiar with the problem of finding toys for her children which are safe for a baby to cuddle and a small child to tug at and play with. Toys which are free from the danger of toxic dyes and colourings, eyes attached with pins and other dangerous 'extras' which could harm a small child.

The Golden Hands Book of Soft Toys to Make for Children will help you to be sure their toys are safe, as well as beautiful and inexpensive. All you need is a little time and patience and some scraps of fabric from your sewing bag. The patterns are all clearly given on graph and come with detailed on-page instructions of fillings, stitches and how to make up the toys. In the first chapter you will find a useful know-how section, on fillings and how to make toys washable or safe for the very young, plus diagrams of all the stitches you will need. This section also explains how to alter the patterns, so that the toy can be made to any size you like. You can make a whole toy box of teddy bears, lions, cats, dolls, puppets, a wigwam, a seal pyjama case . . . over forty lovely toys. Some are traditional, some lifelike and some very modern, but all are easy and quick to make. Many of the toys are even simple enough for a young child to make for himself, one rainy afternoon. The symbols beside each entry on page four indicate whether each toy is simple, very simple or detailed. e.g.

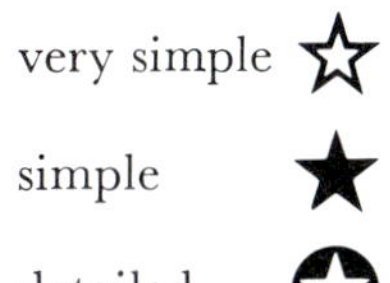

As a rough guide the very simple ones should be easy enough for a child between the ages of 7 and 11 years to make, the simple for children above 11 years, while the detailed ones are best left to teenagers and adults.

There are so many delightful things to make; cuddly (and safe) toys for babies, funny and original toys for older children, amusing puppets, enchanting dolls for a pretty teenage bedroom. In fact toys for every age, well designed to give great and lasting pleasure to you and your children.

contents

Designers

Tessa Reuss, page 17
Sheila Brull, pages 26, 50
Audrey Hersch, pages 28, 34, 55, 58, 64 (left)
Sheila Cockroft, pages 32, 38, 62 (left), 64 (right), 69
Homebound craftsmen, pages 45, 60
Rosemary Cooper, page 62 (right)

Accessories

Kitchen ware by Habitat, page 55

CHRIS LEWIS

know-how

The patterns

The patterns are all on graph. Each square on the graph represents one inch square and seam allowances are included, unless otherwise stated. These seam allowances vary according to the size of toy and fabric used.

Making a pattern from graph

You will need a pencil and graph paper to make the patterns. Alternatively you can place a sheet of greaseproof paper over graph paper and draw the pattern on to the greaseproof paper. Yet another way, recommended for small pattern pieces only, is to draw up a piece of paper accurately into 1-inch squares.

To copy the pattern, say for bodice front, start from top left hand corner of diagram. Count squares to lower point of neck line and mark on paper. Now measure distance of upper point of neck from side and top of paper, mark and connect the two points to copy neck curve. Draw remainder of pattern to scale similarly. Copy all pattern pieces in the same way. Identify every pattern piece—back, front, head, body gusset and so on. Also mark any details, such as centre back or front, darts, notches and any letters.

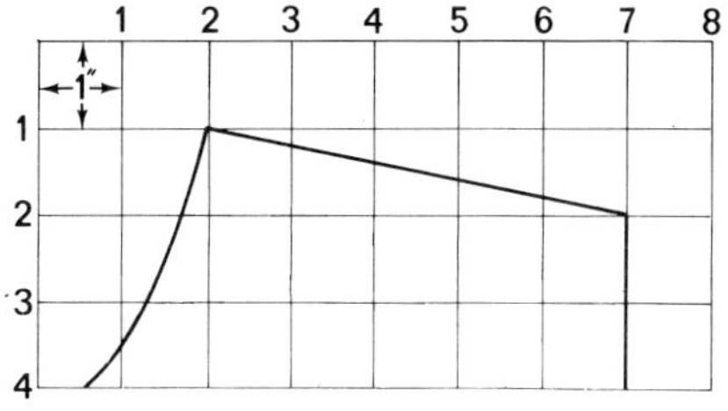

Enlarging a pattern on graph

It is a simple matter to make the graph patterns larger or smaller than the actual patterns given.

If you want to make the patterns twice as large simply interpret the 1-inch grid as being a 2-inch grid and plot the graph on to 2-inch squares. Similarly you can make it $1\frac{1}{2}$ times as large by using a $1\frac{1}{2}$-inch grid, or you can make it smaller by using a $\frac{1}{2}$-inch or $\frac{3}{4}$-inch grid etc.

One word of warning however—the seam allowance gets enlarged or reduced in the same proportion and if you do not take the new seam allowance the toy will be out of proportion. A way of overcoming this is to draw in the stitching line on the original graph then follow the stitching line when drawing out the new pattern size. Add the required seam allowance when you have finished.

Going metric

The patterns are all on 1-inch squares. If inch graph paper is unavailable draw up a piece of paper into 1-inch squares to the size required for the pattern piece. If centimetre graph paper is available it is a good idea to draw that up into 1-inch squares using a contrasting colour. This way the existing grid will help you to get your lines parallel. To save time draw up one piece into inch squares, place tracing paper over it and draw the pattern pieces onto this.

All the fabric requirements are given in yards, the chart below gives you the equivalent in metres.

YARD/METRE CHART

yd	m	yd	m	yd	m	yd	m
$\frac{1}{8}$	0.15	$\frac{7}{8}$	0.80	$1\frac{5}{8}$	1.50	$2\frac{3}{8}$	2.20
$\frac{1}{4}$	0.25	1	0.95	$1\frac{3}{4}$	1.60	$2\frac{1}{2}$	2.30
$\frac{3}{8}$	0.35	$1\frac{1}{8}$	1.05	$1\frac{7}{8}$	1.75	$2\frac{5}{8}$	2.40
$\frac{1}{2}$	0.50	$1\frac{1}{4}$	1.15	2	1.85	$2\frac{3}{4}$	2.55
$\frac{5}{8}$	0.60	$1\frac{3}{8}$	1.30	$2\frac{1}{8}$	1.95	$2\frac{7}{8}$	2.65
$\frac{3}{4}$	0.70	$1\frac{1}{2}$	1.40	$2\frac{1}{4}$	2.10	3	2.75

Cutting out

If the fabric has become creased, press carefully. Leave fabric folded, wrong side out, selvedges together, unless fabric layout suggests alternative folding. Take care with one way fabrics where pattern or pile run in same direction.

Follow the fabric layout where given.

To get a left and right side of a pattern piece when cutting out in single fabric, you will need to place the pattern first with the right side of pattern facing upwards then turn pattern over and cut a second piece with the wrong side of the pattern facing upwards.

Fur fabric

Cutting out: Fur fabric has a woven or knitted backing. In either case lay the fabric pile side down, and cut one layer at a time, keeping pattern pieces on straight grain of backing. Mark round pattern pieces with tailor's chalk and cut backing with sharp scissors or blade, taking care not to cut the pile.

Stitching: Stitch with a strong needle and a thread with elasticity such as a pure silk or synthetic thread. Experiment on scraps for stitch tension. Separate hairs of pile before stitching. When stitched use a pin to ease out pile along seam line.

Fillings

There are several alternatives for filling soft toys. Kapok gives a very firm filling but it is not washable. So do be sure before you use it that you will not want to wash the toy. Synthetic wadding fillings, on the other hand, are washable but do not pack as firmly as kapok.

An alternative to the above is foam pieces. These are washable but they can provide quite a lumpy finish unless the fabric is very firm. Foam pieces are best used on large toys, such as the giant snail, which would take vast quantities of a synthetic wadding filling.

Two other fillings recommended in this book are sawdust, used for pin cushions, and wood wool. Both give a very hard, firm finish but they are not washable.

Safe toys

For young children make sure that the toys you make are quite free from anything that could cause injury. Substitute embroidered eyes for buttons and do not include anything with wire in it.

Safety eyes: Special safety glass eyes can be bought at most toy-making departments. These are not the ones with wires which get pushed into the fabric and which can then be pulled out. Safety eyes come with a little stalk which gets pushed through the fabric to the wrong side. Over the stalk is hammered a piece of metal a bit like an eyelet which sandwiches the fabric between the eye in the front and the metal disc inside.

stitch library

Back stitch

Bring the thread through on the stitching line, then take a small backward stitch through the fabric. Bring the needle through again a little in front of the first stitch. Then take another stitch, inserting the needle at the point where the first stitch came through.

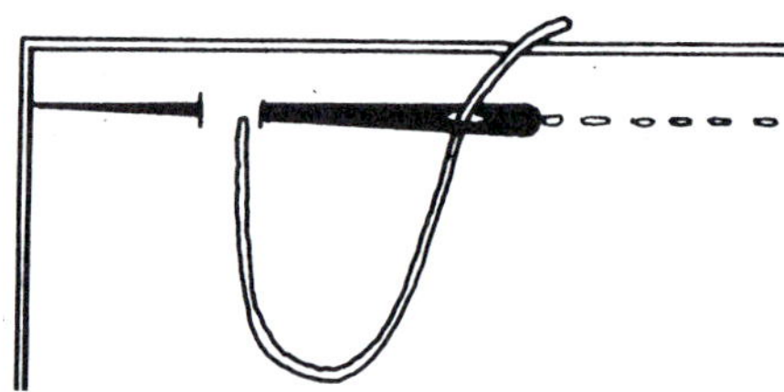

Blanket stitch

The thread loops underneath the needle which lies vertically in the fabric.

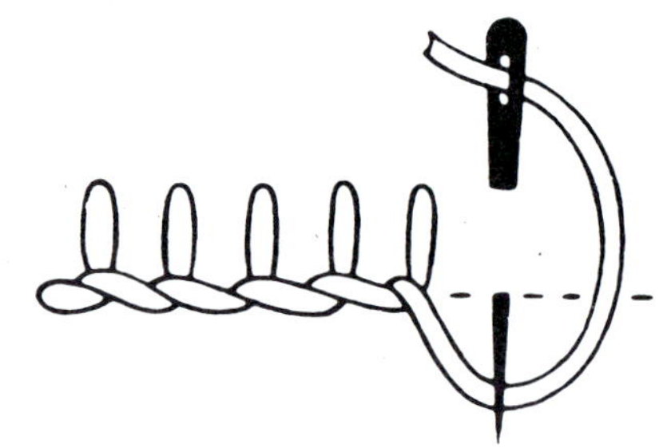

Buttonhole stitch

The knot is tighter than blanket stitch and is pulled up to the top of the stitch.

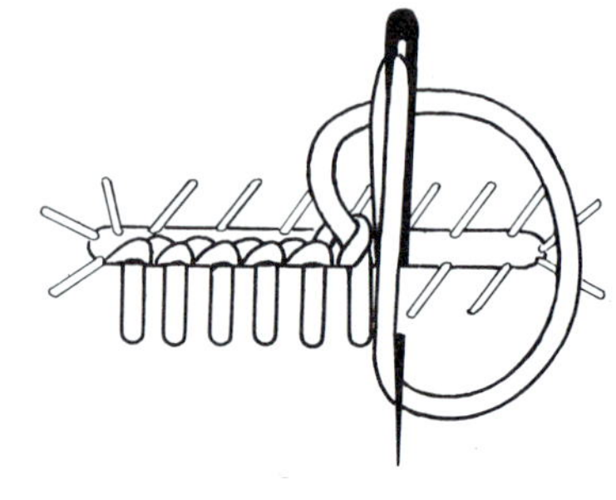

Chain stitch

Work from right to left, making a chain of loops on the right side of the fabric. The needle returns to the place where it came out, the thread looping under it. Do not pull too tight.

Couching

Lay a loose thread on the fabric and, with another thread, catch it to the fabric at intervals with small stitches.

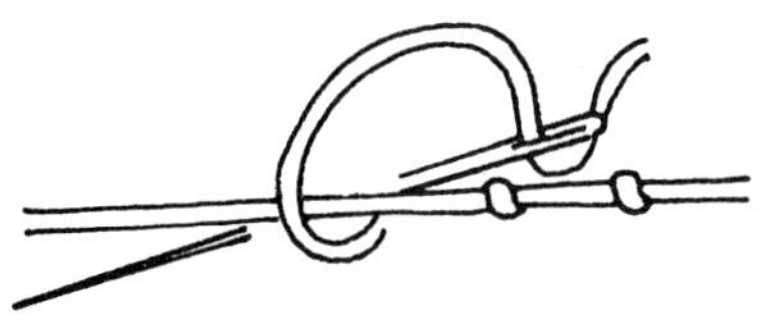

Double cross stitch

Work a single cross then work another cross between the axis of the first cross as in the diagram (**A**). A small stitch can also be sewn over the centre, (diagram **B**).

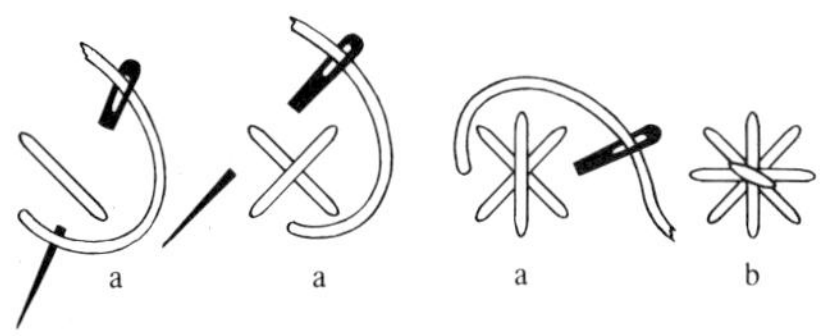

Draw stitch or Ladder stitch

To pull two parallel edges invisibly together. Make stitches alternately through the folds on each side of the opening, pulling up so that no thread is seen.

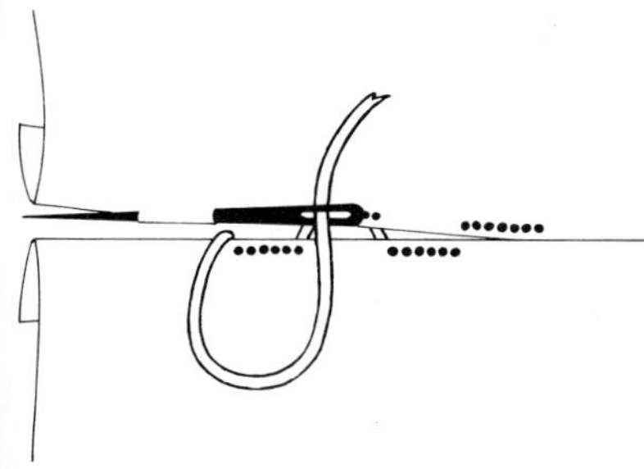

Fly stitch

Make a straight stitch from left to right, holding it down with the left thumb. Bring the needle out again a little below the centre of the stitch and secure in a 'V' shape with a small downward stitch.

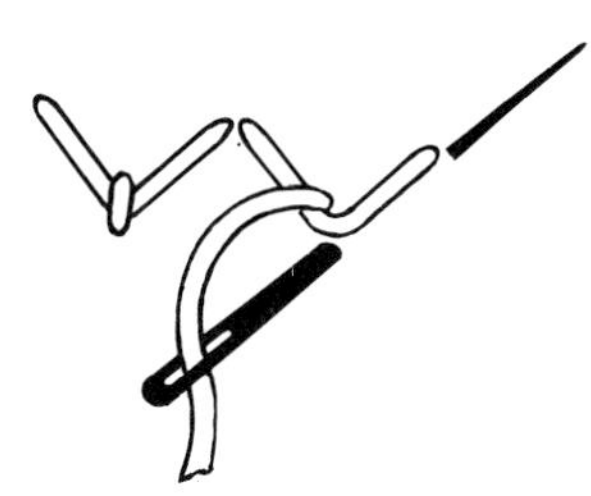

French knots

Bring the thread through the fabric, hold down with the left thumb and encircle the thread twice with the needle, as in **A**. Insert the needle beside the point where it emerged and pull through.

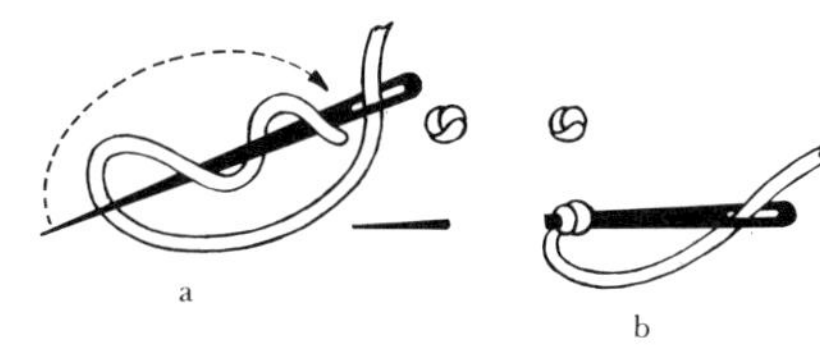

Oversewing stitch

This stitch is used on raw edges to prevent them fraying. Working from either direction make diagonal, evenly spaced, stitches over the edge.

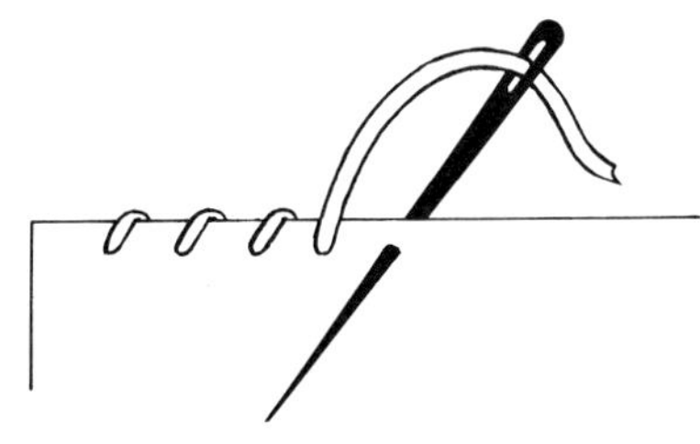

Running stitch

Weave needle in and out of fabric before pulling through. Several stitches can be made on needle at same time. Draw up stitches if gathers are required.

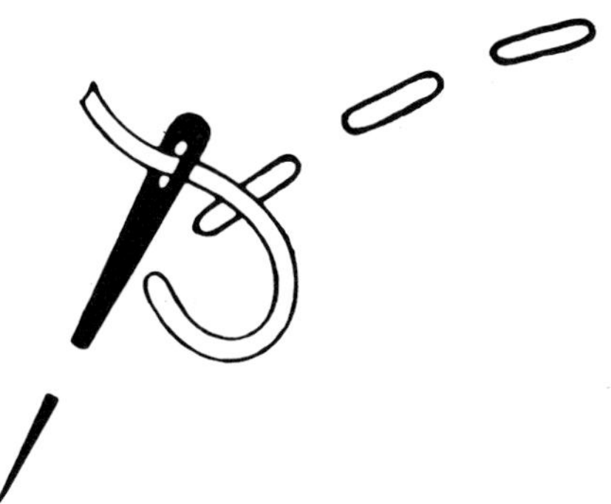

Satin stitch

Work straight stitches closely together across the required shape. The stitches should be of even tension and not too long.

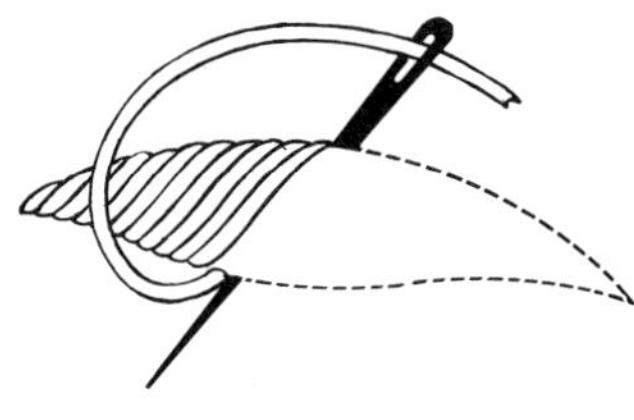

Slip stitch

To invisibly join a turned-in edge to the right side of body. Working from right to left take a stitch through body and then pass along the turned-in edge for $\frac{1}{8}$ to $\frac{1}{4}$ inch.

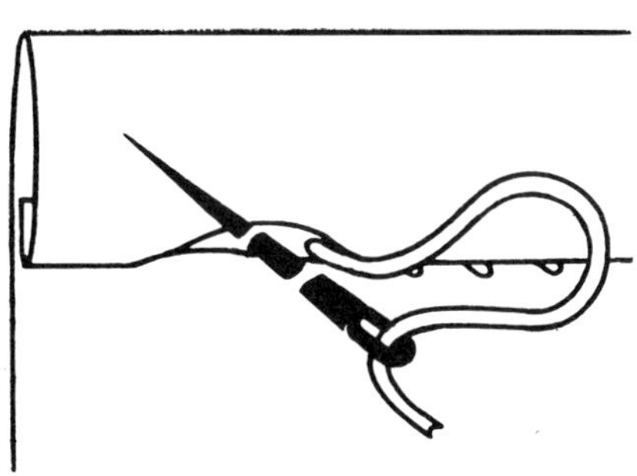

Stab stitch

This stitch holds fabric layers together very firmly and is worked from right to left. Working from one side push needle down vertically, pull needle through from other side. Then push needle up vertically and pull through from top side. The stitches should be very small.

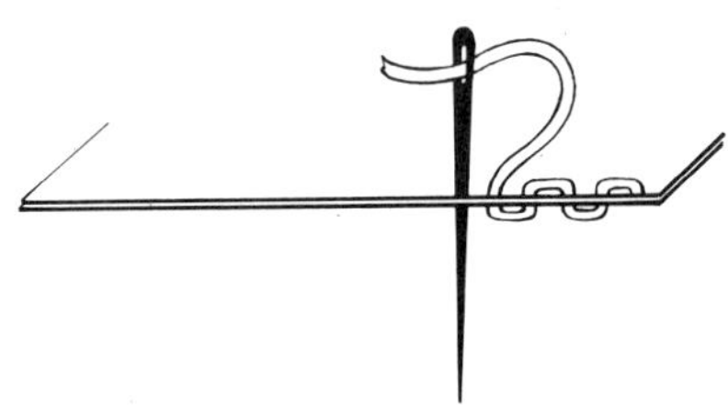

Stem stitch

Work from left to right, taking regular, slightly slanting stitches along the line of the design. The thread always emerges on the left side of the previous stitch. Use for flower stems, outlines etc.

CAMERA PRESS

salami the sausage dog

Gay gingham sausage dogs, about 2 foot long, make great playmates. They can be made all in one fabric or with contrasting face, ears and underbody.

Materials required

For each dog you will need:
$\frac{1}{2}$ yard 36-inch wide gingham fabric
$\frac{1}{4}$ yard 36-inch wide contrast fabric (or gingham as above)
Foam pieces or synthetic wadding for filling
Scraps felt, buttons or embroidery thread for eyes

To make pattern

See Know-How.
The pattern pieces you will need are:
1. Body (cut 2); **2.** Underbody (cut 1 on fold); **3.** Head gusset (cut 1); **4.** Ear (cut 4).

To cut out

Follow the cutting layouts. The pattern has $\frac{1}{4}$-inch seam allowance included.
Note the body (**1**) and two ear pieces (**4**) are cut from gingham fabric. The underbody (**2**), head gusset (**3**) and two ear pieces (**4**) are cut from contrast fabric.

Making up

All seams are stitched with right sides together, unless otherwise stated.
Take $\frac{1}{4}$-inch seams throughout.
Arrange gingham and plain ear pieces together in pairs. Stitch round outer curved edge from A to B. Turn to right side. Position an ear to right side of each body piece, with contrast fabric facing gingham, raw edges level. Tack in place.
Stitch head gusset between the two body pieces from nose to top of head (AC), including the ears in the seam.
Sew body pieces together from D to A and E to C.
Position underbody to body and stitch all round leaving a 3 inch opening along one side for turning.
Turn right side out and stuff firmly. Turn in seam allowance along opening and draw stitch to close.
Sew on eyes as in the picture.
The dog can be decorated with hearts or simply left plain.

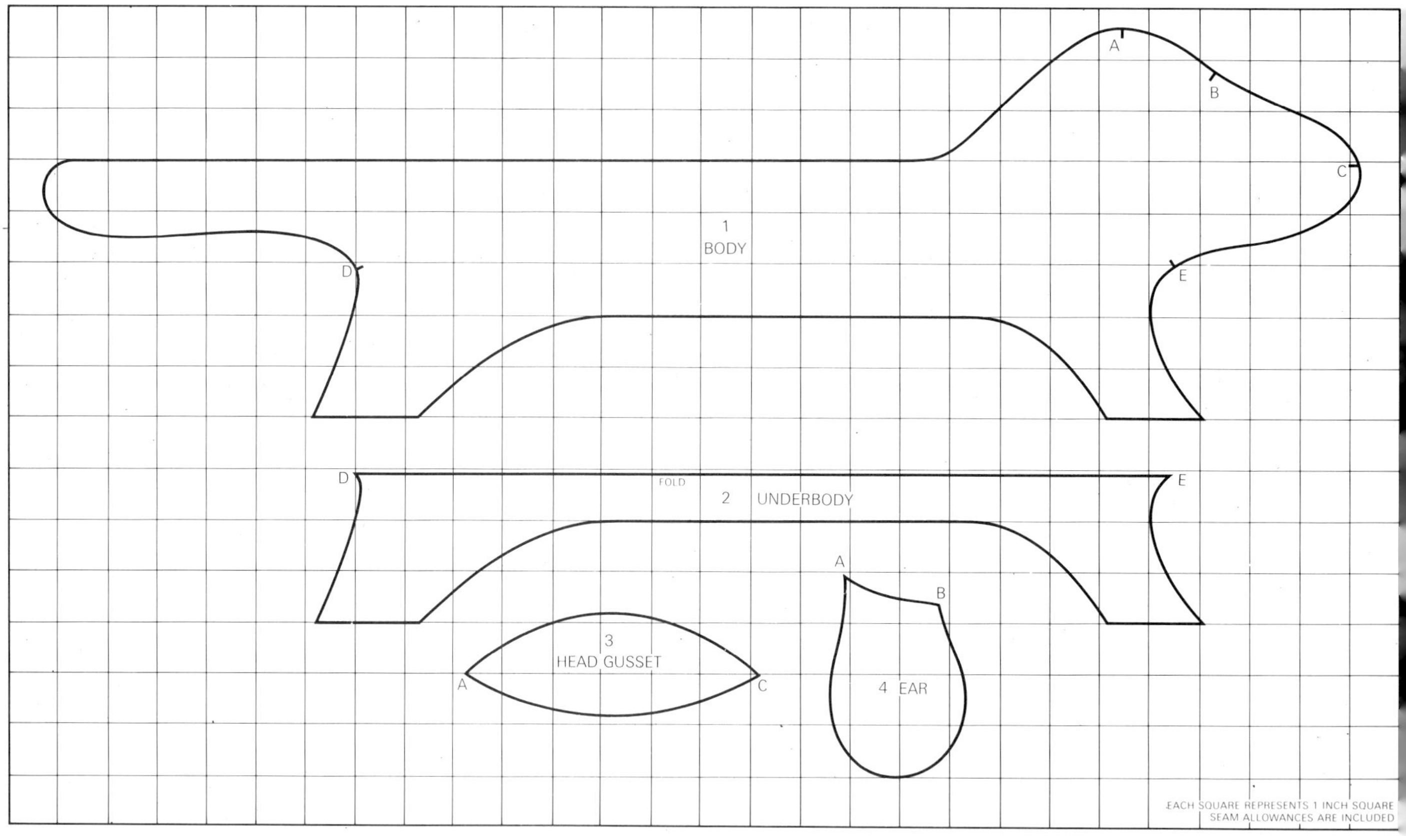

A B C D E
1 BODY
D E FOLD 2 UNDERBODY
3 HEAD GUSSET A C
A B 4 EAR
EACH SQUARE REPRESENTS 1 INCH SQUARE
SEAM ALLOWANCES ARE INCLUDED

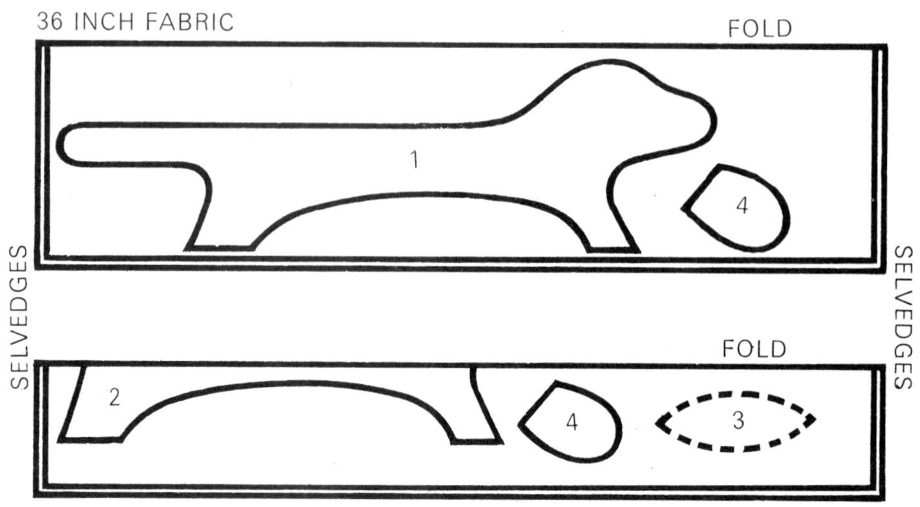

osimoff the owl

Osimoff is an amazing bird with multi-coloured wings, standing 8 inches high. His exotic looks come from the patchwork wings, for which you can use up any scraps of fabric—we used towelling.

Materials required

$\frac{1}{2}$ yard 36-inch wide plain fabric
Coloured remnants of terry towelling
Two $\frac{1}{2}$-inch diameter ball buttons for eyes
Six $\frac{1}{4}$-inch diameter ball buttons for claws
Synthetic wadding for filling

To make pattern

See Know-How.
The pattern pieces you will need are:
1. Body (cut 1 on fold); **2.** Eye pieces (3 shapes, cut 2 of each); **3.** Nose (two parts, cut 1 of each); **4.** Wings (cut 2); **5.** Patchwork diamond (cut 32).

To cut out

Follow the cutting layout. The pattern has $\frac{1}{4}$ inch seam allowance included.
The eye and nose pieces and patchwork diamonds for the wings are cut from the terry towelling remants, the rest is cut from plain fabric.

Making up

All seams are stitched right sides together, taking $\frac{1}{4}$-inch seams, unless otherwise stated.
Using the zig-zag stitch on the machine, stitch the patchwork diamonds together following Figure 1.
Cut out the wing shape in the patchwork and zig-zag the patchwork wing piece to the plain wing piece, wrong sides together.
Using the zig-zag stitch again, stitch eye pieces in position as indicated on pattern.
Stitch centre front seam AB leaving a 3-inch opening for turning. Match E to A at head and stitch from H to AE to H.
Match B to C at base and stitch edges together similarly. Turn to right side and stuff firmly. Close front seam with invisible draw stitches.
Slipstitch the wings to the body from F to G as indicated on pattern and picture.
Place the nose pieces together, matching notches and stitch from J to K to L. Turn to right side. Turn under seam allowance and fill lightly. Slipstitch to the body as in picture.
Sew on two ball buttons for the eyes and three ball buttons for each foot.
At either side of head at H draw out the material into a little flap, and sew flat to form 'ear', using stab stitches along base of 'ear'.

CAMERA PRESS

See patterns overleaf

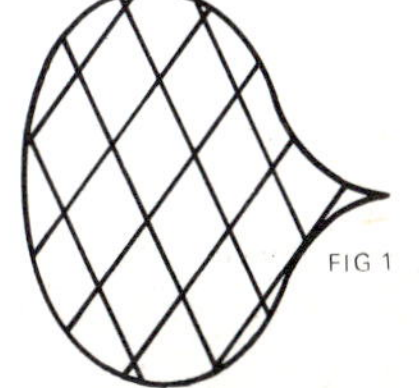
FIG 1

snuffles the hound

Snuffles is a hound dog, 12 inches long, with drooping ears. He can be used as a pillow or taken exploring. Snuffles will be a faithful friend.

Materials required

$\frac{1}{4}$ yard 36-inch wide plain fabric
$\frac{1}{2}$ yard 36-inch wide patterned fabric
Scrap of contrast fabric for nose
One $\frac{1}{2}$-inch diameter ball button for nose
Two $\frac{1}{2}$-inch diameter buttons for eyes
Synthetic wadding for filling

To make pattern

See Know-How.
The pattern pieces you will need are: **1.** Head (cut 1 on fold); **2.** Body (cut 1 on fold); **3.** Ear (cut 4); **4.** Nose (cut 1); **5.** Paw (cut 4).

To cut out

Follow the cutting layouts. The pattern includes a $\frac{1}{2}$-inch seam allowance. Note that the body is cut from patterned fabric, the head, ears, paws and tail from plain fabric and the nose from a scrap of contrast fabric. For the tail cut a strip of material 8 inches by $2\frac{1}{2}$ inches.

Making up

All seams are stitched with right sides together, unless otherwise stated.
Stitch body piece to head piece along ABA.
Stitch ear pieces together in pairs, leaving straight edge open. Turn to right side.
Position an ear to each side of the head on the right side, with AC's matching and raw edges level. Tack in place.
Stitch centre back seam EAD including ears inside the seam and leaving a 4-inch opening for turning.
Working at the top, bring F to meet E and stitch to straight head edge from G to EF to G. Working at the base bring H to meet D and stitch similarly.
Turn right side out and stuff firmly. Close the back seam opening with invisible draw stitches.
Turn in seam allowance on nose piece and slipstitch to head as indicated on pattern. Attach paws similarly in position.
Sew on buttons for eyes and nose.
Fold the tail piece lengthwise, right sides together, and stitch edges leaving one narrow end open. Turn out and fill lightly with filling. Turn in seam allowance and stitch firmly to body at D.

oscar the cat

Oscar is a very simple animal to make. If the whiskers are left off and he is filled with foam pieces, Oscar becomes an ideal washable flat toy for a very small child. Oscar is about 9 inches high.

Materials required

$\frac{1}{2}$ yard 36-inch wide main fabric
$\frac{1}{4}$ yard 36-inch wide contrasting fabric
Embroidery cottons in red, yellow and green
One packet of whiskers
Synthetic wadding or foam pieces for filling

To make pattern

See Know-How.
The pattern pieces you will need are: **1.** Body (cut 1 on fold); **2.** Ear (cut 4); **3.** Leg (cut 4); **4.** Tail (cut 2).

To cut out

Follow the cutting layouts. The pattern has $\frac{1}{4}$-inch seam allowance included.
The body is cut from the main fabric and the ears, paws and tail from contrasting fabric.

Making up

All seams are stitched with right sides together taking $\frac{1}{4}$-inch seams, unless otherwise stated.
Stitch centre back seam AB leaving a 3-inch opening for turning.
At the top, bring C to meet A and stitch curved edge to straight edge from D to AC to D. At the base bring E to meet B and stitch similarly.
Turn right side out and stuff firmly. Turn in seam allowance at opening and draw stitch to close.
Stitch ears in pairs leaving straight edges open. Turn to right side and turn in seam allowance on straight edges. Make a small pleat in each ear as in the picture, then firmly slipstitch an ear to each side of the head at D.
Stitch legs together in pairs leaving bottom edge open. Turn to right side, turn in seam allowance on open edge and fill lightly. Slipstitch to base of body as in picture.
Place tail pieces together and stitch long edges and rounded end. Turn right side out and fill lightly. Turn in seam allowance at open end and slipstitch this edge to base of centre back seam. Wrap the tail around the cat as shown and stitch to body at the front with invisible slip stitches.
Embroider the face of the cat and the claws, and sew on whiskers, following the picture.

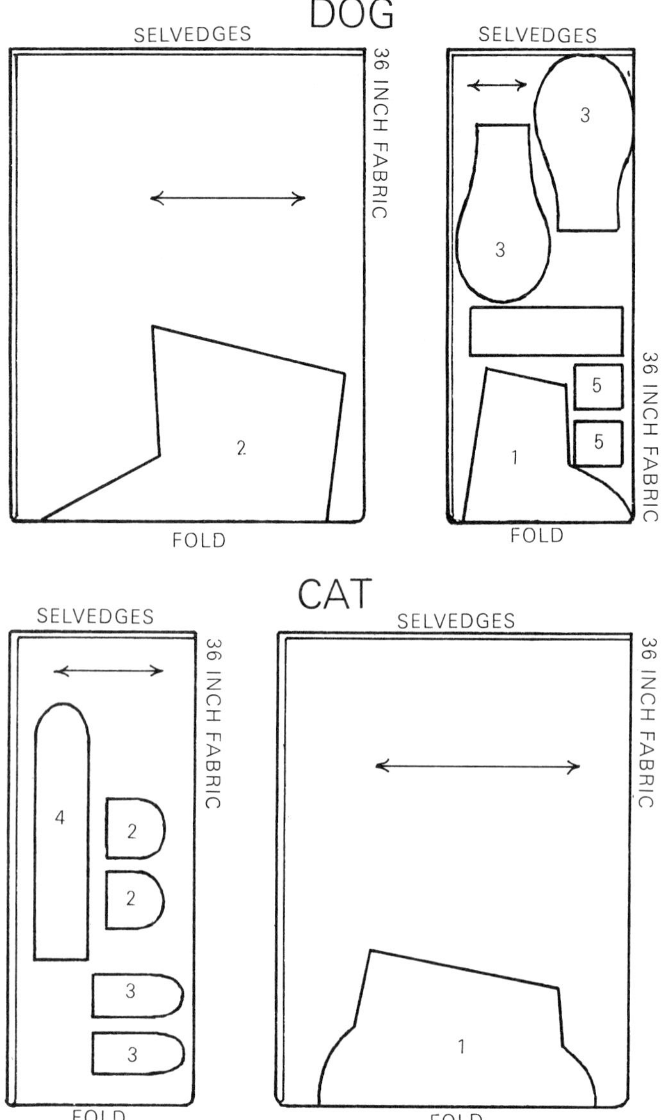

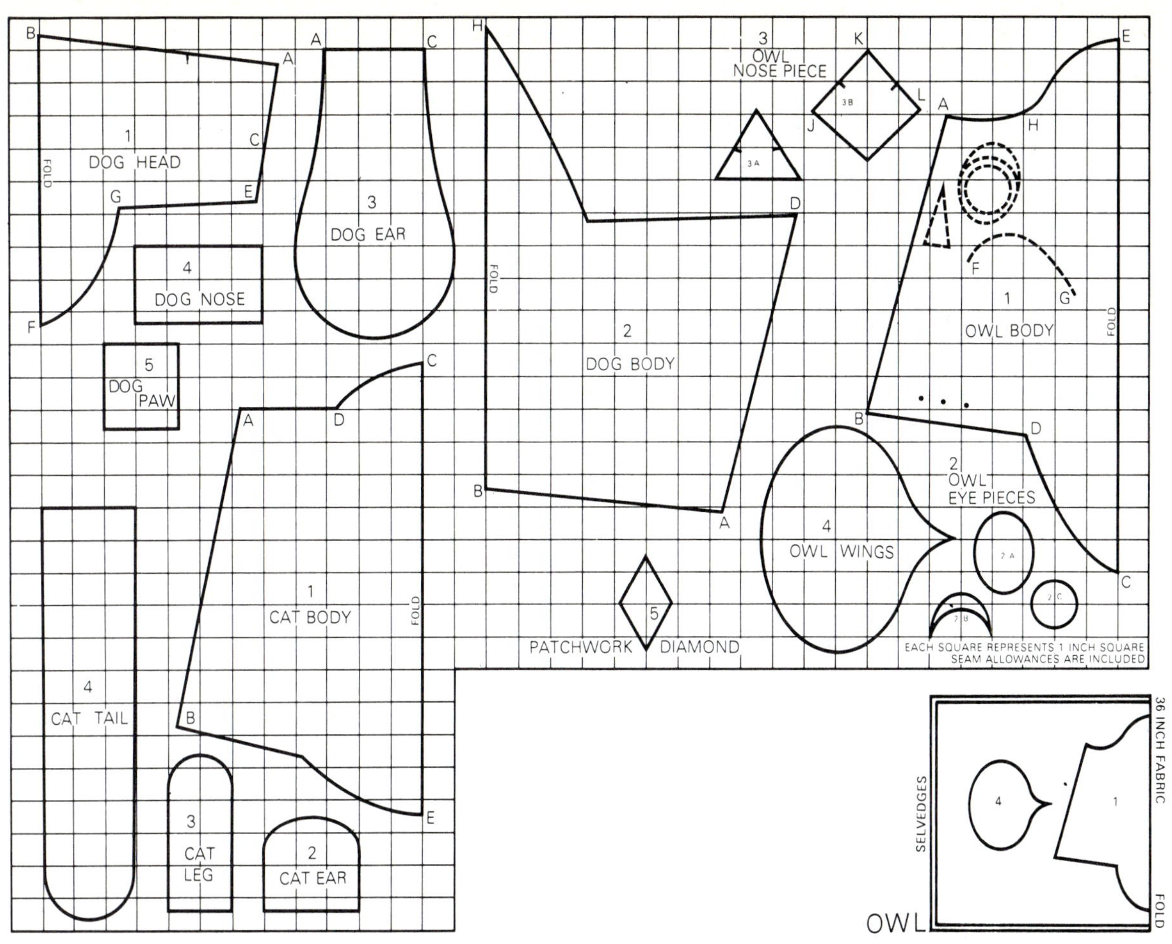

BETA PICTURES

felix, felicity and flip

This cat trio of father, mother and baby will charm cat lovers of all ages. They are made from terry towelling and vary in length from 13 to 18 inches.

Materials required

$\frac{1}{2}$ yard 36-inch wide terry towelling for kitten
$\frac{5}{8}$ yard 36-inch wide terry towelling for mother cat
1 yard 36-inch wide terry towelling for father cat
Scraps black and white felt
Scraps black and white wool for features
Kapok or synthetic wadding for filling
Fabric adhesive

To make pattern

The pattern pieces you will need are: **1.** Head Kitten (cut 2); **2.** Body Kitten (cut 2); **3.** Head Mother (cut 2); **4.** Body Mother (cut 2); **5.** Head Father (cut 2); **6.** Body Father (cut 2).

To cut out

Cut each pattern piece from double terry towelling. Remember you need a back and front for each.
From felt cut out features as in the picture.

Making up

For each cat: All seams are stitched with right sides together, taking $\frac{1}{4}$-inch seams.
Stitch body pieces together all round, leaving AB open.
Turn to right side and stuff firmly. Turn in seam allowance at opening and close.
Assemble eye pieces and stick together with fabric adhesive. Stick to face, stick on remaining felt features and embroider the rest of the face.
Sew head pieces together, leaving opening between DC.
Turn to right side and stuff firmly. Turn in seam allowance at opening and ladder stitch to close.
Lay head over top left hand corner of body and, using wool, blanket stitch to body.

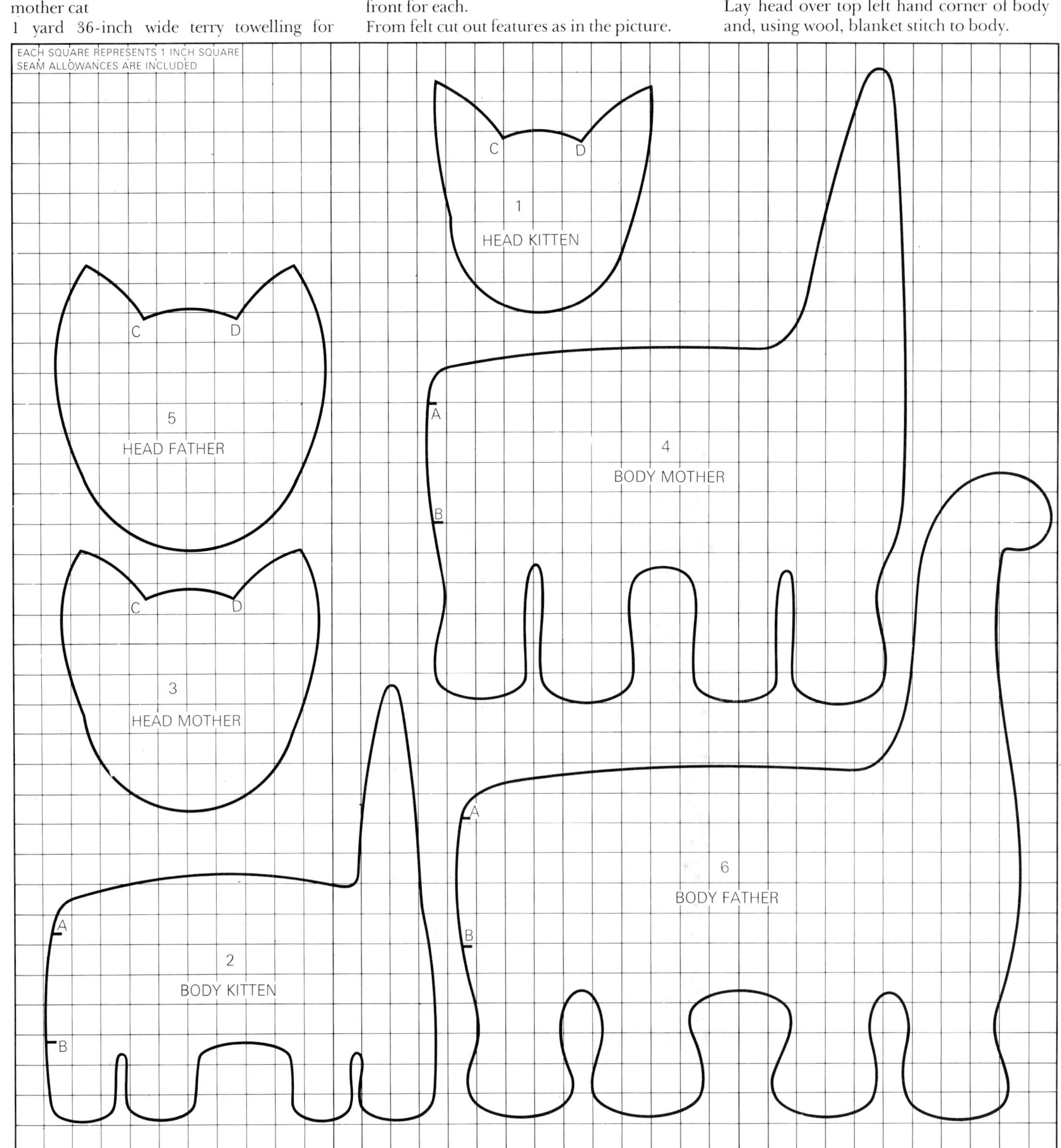

CHRIS LEWIS

miss mouse

Here is Miss Mouse, 6 inches high, keeping Moppet at bay.

Materials required

White Acrilan fur fabric 10 inches by 7 inches
6-inch square pink felt
$\frac{1}{2}$ yard $\frac{1}{2}$-inch wide ribbon
Two $\frac{3}{8}$ inch diameter safety glass eyes
Synthetic wadding or foam pieces for filling
Fabric adhesive
Pink embroidery cotton

To make pattern

See Know-How.
The pattern pieces you will need are:
1. Body (cut 2). Also make separate patterns for feet (cut 4) and paws (cut 4) from body pattern.

To cut out

The pattern has $\frac{1}{4}$-inch seam allowance included where necessary.
Place body pattern on double thickness of fur fabric and cut out. Also cut two $1\frac{1}{2}$-inch diameter circles in fur fabric for ears.
From felt cut four paws and four feet, two $1\frac{1}{2}$-inch diameter circles for ears and a piece $1\frac{1}{4}$ inches by 6 inches for tail. Taper long sides of tail so that one end is $\frac{5}{8}$ inch wide.

Making up

All seams are stitched with right sides together, taking $\frac{1}{4}$-inch seams, unless otherwise stated.
Stitch body pieces together leaving a 2-inch opening at base. Turn to right side.
Insert eyes on each side of head.
Fill head and body firmly. Oversew body opening to close.
Using fabric adhesive stick felt ear pieces to wrong side of Acrilan ear pieces. Fold each ear with pink side inwards and oversew firmly to head as illustrated.
Stick paw and foot pieces together in pairs. Sew the straight sides of each paw and foot to body.
Fold tail in half and oversew long edges together. Sew wide end of tail to base of body.
Embroider nose and whiskers on face.
Tie ribbon round neck.

See picture overleaf

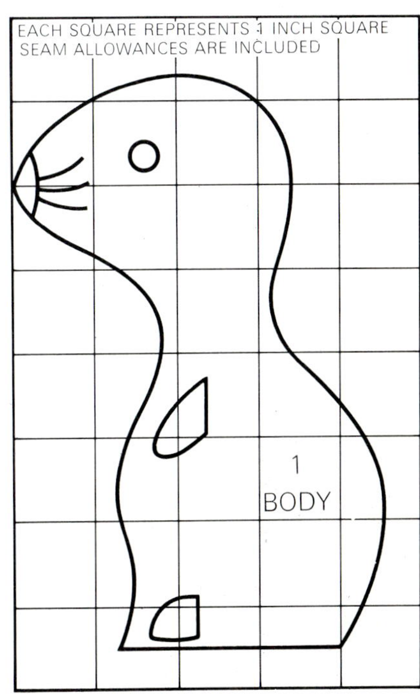

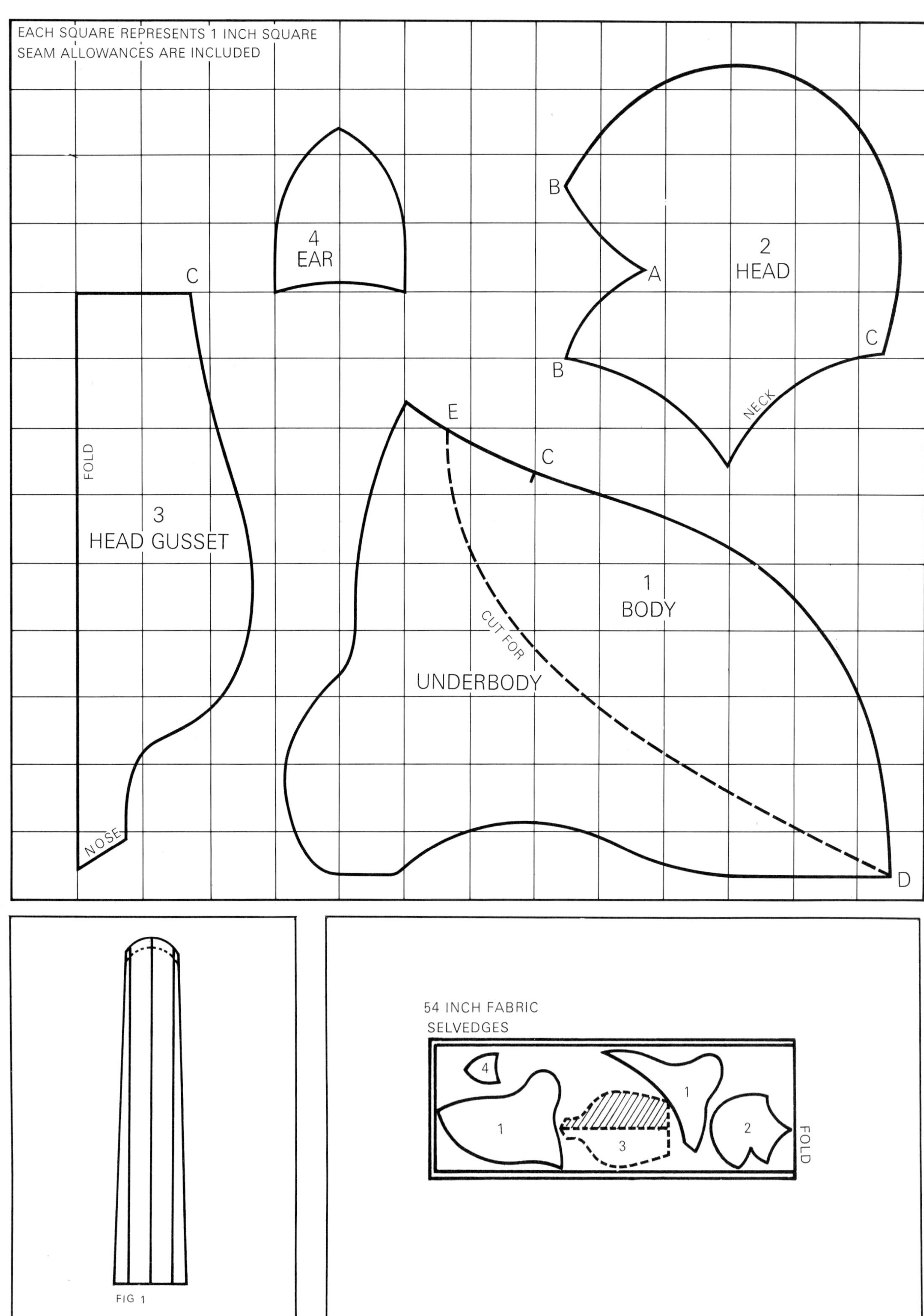
EACH SQUARE REPRESENTS 1 INCH SQUARE
SEAM ALLOWANCES ARE INCLUDED
4
EAR
B
A
2
HEAD
C
B
NECK
C
FOLD
3
HEAD GUSSET
NOSE
E
C
1
BODY
CUT FOR
UNDERBODY
D
FIG 1
54 INCH FABRIC
SELVEDGES
4
1
1
3
2
FOLD

moppet the pussy cat

Moppet is a cuddly white pussy cat who is 11 inches high. She purrs and catches mice—in fact she does everything a pussy cat should do.

Materials required

$\frac{1}{4}$ yard 54-inch wide Acrilan fur fabric
$\frac{3}{4}$ yard 1-inch wide ribbon
Scraps of pink and black felt
Two glass eyes (use felt if for a young child)
Bell
Washable wadding for filling
Black and red embroidery cotton
Fabric adhesive

To make pattern

See Know-How.
The pattern pieces you will need are: **1.** Body (cut 2); **2.** Head (cut 2); **3.** Head gusset (cut 1 on fold); **4.** Ear (cut 4).
Also make a pattern for the underbody following dotted line on body piece.

To cut out

The pattern has $\frac{1}{4}$-inch seam allowance included.
See cutting layout for fur fabric. Also cut a piece of fur fabric 8 inches by $4\frac{1}{2}$ inches for tail. Note that both complete body section (**1**) and underbody are cut from double fabric.
Cut two inner ears from pink felt.

Making up

All seams are stitched with right sides together and $\frac{1}{4}$-inch seams unless otherwise stated.
Make darts on head pieces, sewing from A to B. Insert head gusset between head pieces, starting at point C and sewing over head from C to nose.
Sew centre of face together from nose to chin, leaving neck edge open. Turn to right side.
Half fill and if using glass eyes, push them into head and twist wires together. Fill rest of head firmly.
Stick pink felt inner ears to wrong side of outer ears. Oversew short edge of each completed ear to top of head.
Sew body pieces together from C to D. Sew underbody pieces together from E to D along inner edge.
Sew underbody piece between body sides, matching points E and D. Trim corners, turn to right side and fill firmly.
Ease neck edge of head into top of body and oversew head and body together.
Taper long sides of tail piece so that one narrow edge measures 3 inches. Fold tail lengthways and sew long edges together. Flatten tail so that seam is centred. Round off narrow end and stitch to close (see Figure 1). Turn to right side and fill.
Cover tip of tail with $1\frac{1}{2}$ inch by 3 inch piece of black felt and stitch to secure.
Sew tail to base of body with seam side uppermost. Catch seam to back of body for about 2 inches.
Embroider nose and mouth in red and whiskers and claws in black. Stick on black felt eyes if required.
Thread bell on ribbon and tie round neck.

CONWAY PICTURE LIBRARY

BETA PICTURES

hop, skip and jump

This dramatic cat and mouse trio is very simple to make but beautiful in black and blue velvet. The cat is about 18 inches high and the well-fed mice from 8 to 10 inches long.

Materials required

For cat:
$1\frac{1}{4}$ yard 36-inch wide black velvet or velveteen
One 9-inch square of grey felt and one of white felt
1 yard of 2-inch wide ribbon for bow
Copydex or other fabric adhesive
Synthetic wadding for filling

For two mice: (one large, one small)
$\frac{1}{4}$ yard 36-inch wide blue velvet or velveteen
One 9-inch square of grey felt
$\frac{1}{4}$ yard 1-inch wide black leather binding
Four small black ball buttons for eyes
Synthetic wadding for filling

To make pattern

See Know-How.
The pattern pieces you will need are:
1. Cat (cut 2); **2.** Mouse—large (cut 2); **3.** Mouse—small (cut 2); **4.** Mouse ears (cut 4).

To cut out

Follow the cutting layouts. The pattern has $\frac{1}{2}$-inch seam allowances included where necessary.
The cat: Cut out large eye pieces, nose, whiskers, mouth and paws in grey felt, trimming the eyes with pinking shears. Cut eye whites and claws in white felt.
Mice: Cut leather into $\frac{1}{8}$-inch wide strips 8 inches long for tails and 4 inches long for whiskers. Cut ears in grey felt.

Making up

All seams are stitched with right sides together taking $\frac{1}{2}$-inch seams, unless otherwise stated.
Cat: Stitch back and front cat pieces together, leaving a 4-inch opening for turning. Turn to right side and stuff, taking care that the tail is filled firmly.
Close the opening with ladder stitch.
On the right side of one body piece firmly stick the eyes, nose, mouth, whiskers and paws in place.
Paint or colour in the pupils of the eyes with felt-tip pen.
Tie the ribbon round the cat's neck in a bow.
Mice: On each mouse place body pieces together and stitch all round leaving a 2-inch opening for turning. Turn to right side

d stuff firmly. Close openings with small
der stitches.
ld each ear in half lengthways, and stitch
inted end to mouse's head with small slip-
ches, as in picture.
v on black beads for eyes.
t two 4-inch strips of leather for whiskers.
tch the centres of the whiskers to the
derside of the head with firm oversewing
ches.
tch the tail in position, opening the seam
the base a little to set it in. Slipstitch
mly together.

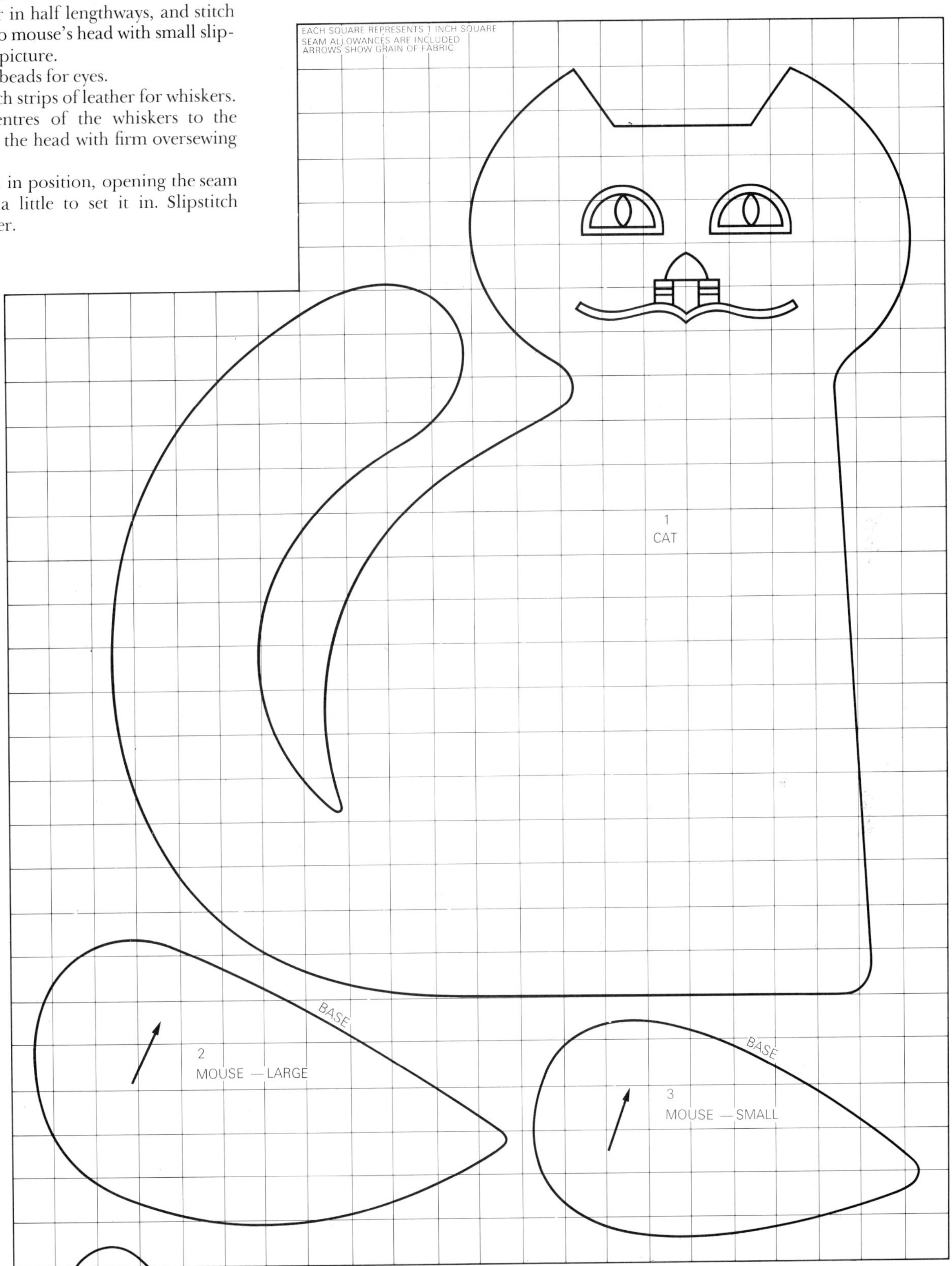

EACH SQUARE REPRESENTS 1 INCH SQUARE
SEAM ALLOWANCES ARE INCLUDED
ARROWS SHOW GRAIN OF FABRIC

1
CAT

BASE
2
MOUSE — LARGE

BASE
3
MOUSE — SMALL

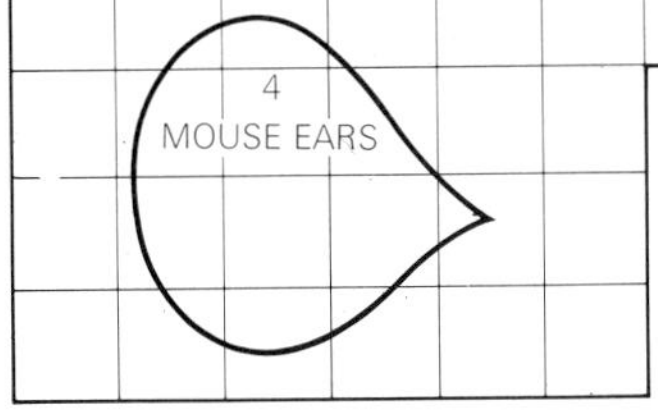

4
MOUSE EARS

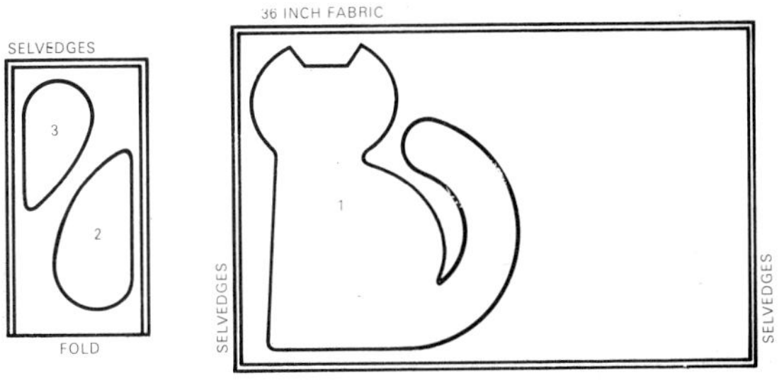

SELVEDGES
3
2
FOLD

36 INCH FABRIC
SELVEDGES
1
SELVEDGES

the yellow squares

A collection of unusual creatures made from yellow towelling and string. They are designed to encourage you to experiment and create your own variations.
Our versions roughly resemble girl and boy twins, a cat, a troll and a fox. The girl and boy twins can be made separate or Siamese from one piece.
Make them larger for cushions or smaller for pincushions or bean bags. Embroider the eyes to make them ideal soft toys for children.

Materials required

Girl twin: $\frac{1}{4}$ yard 36-inch wide yellow towelling
3 yards of string
A mattress needle
3 buttons for the eyes and mouth
Kapok for filling
Boy twin: $\frac{1}{4}$ yard 36-inch wide yellow towelling
2 yards of string
2 buttons for the eyes
Kapok for filling
Siamese twins: The sum of the separate quantities above.
Cat: $\frac{1}{4}$ yard 36-inch wide yellow towelling
Scrap of string
2 buttons for the eyes
Kapok for filling
Troll: $\frac{1}{4}$ yard 36-inch wide yellow towelling
4 yards of string
4 buttons for eyes and front
Kapok for filling
Fox: $\frac{3}{8}$ yard 36-inch wide yellow towelling
$\frac{1}{2}$ yard of string
1 small shiny ball buttons for the eyes
Kapok for filling

To make pattern

Follow the detailed scale layouts carefully.
The pattern pieces you will need are based on squares and strips of material which can be cut as follows:
Twin (for each): **1.** Body—a piece 14 inches by 7 inches; **2.** Legs—two 5-inch squares; **3.** Arms—two pieces 3 inches by 6 inches, rounded at each end.
Siamese twins: 2 and **3** as above for each twin; a combined body piece 28 inches by 7 inches.
Cat: 4. Body—a piece 28 by 7 inches; **5.** Tail—a strip 28 inches by 2 inches; **6.** Ears—two pieces 3 inches by 6 inches rounded at each end.
Troll: 7. Body—a piece 28 inches by 7 inches; **8.** Legs—four pieces 2 inches by 8 inches.
Fox: 9. Body—a piece 28 inches by 7 inches; **10.** Tail—a strip 28 inches by $1\frac{1}{2}$ inches; **11.** Feet—two 5-inch squares; **12.** Head—two triangles $4\frac{1}{2}$ inches by 8 inches; **13.** Ears—four pieces $2\frac{1}{2}$ inches wide, rounded at one end, cut alongside the head triangles following the layout.

To cut out

The pattern includes a $\frac{1}{4}$-inch seam allowance. The pattern layouts are drawn accurately and to scale. The pieces fit neatly into the yardages given and should be cut exactly as indicated.

Making up

All seams are stitched with right sides together, taking $\frac{1}{4}$-inch seams, unless otherwise stated.

Twin (each)
Fold the leg pieces double along the dotted pattern line and stitch the long edges and one end. Turn to the right side and stuff.
Fold the arm pieces double and stitch round leaving a 1-inch opening. Turn to the right side and slipstitch opening to close.
Fold the body piece double on the dotted pattern line and tack the arms and legs in position inside the seam, raw edges level. Stitch around the three sides leaving a 2-inch opening. Turn to the right side and stuff. Slipstitch opening to close.
The girl: Thread the string into a mattress needle and sew it in large loops around the head as in the photograph, making each loop fast with a back stitch. Sew on two buttons for eyes and one for the mouth.
The boy: Cut the cord into 6-inch lengths, make into a neat bundle, and tie firmly in the middle. Stitch the middle of the bundle to the centre of the top body edge.

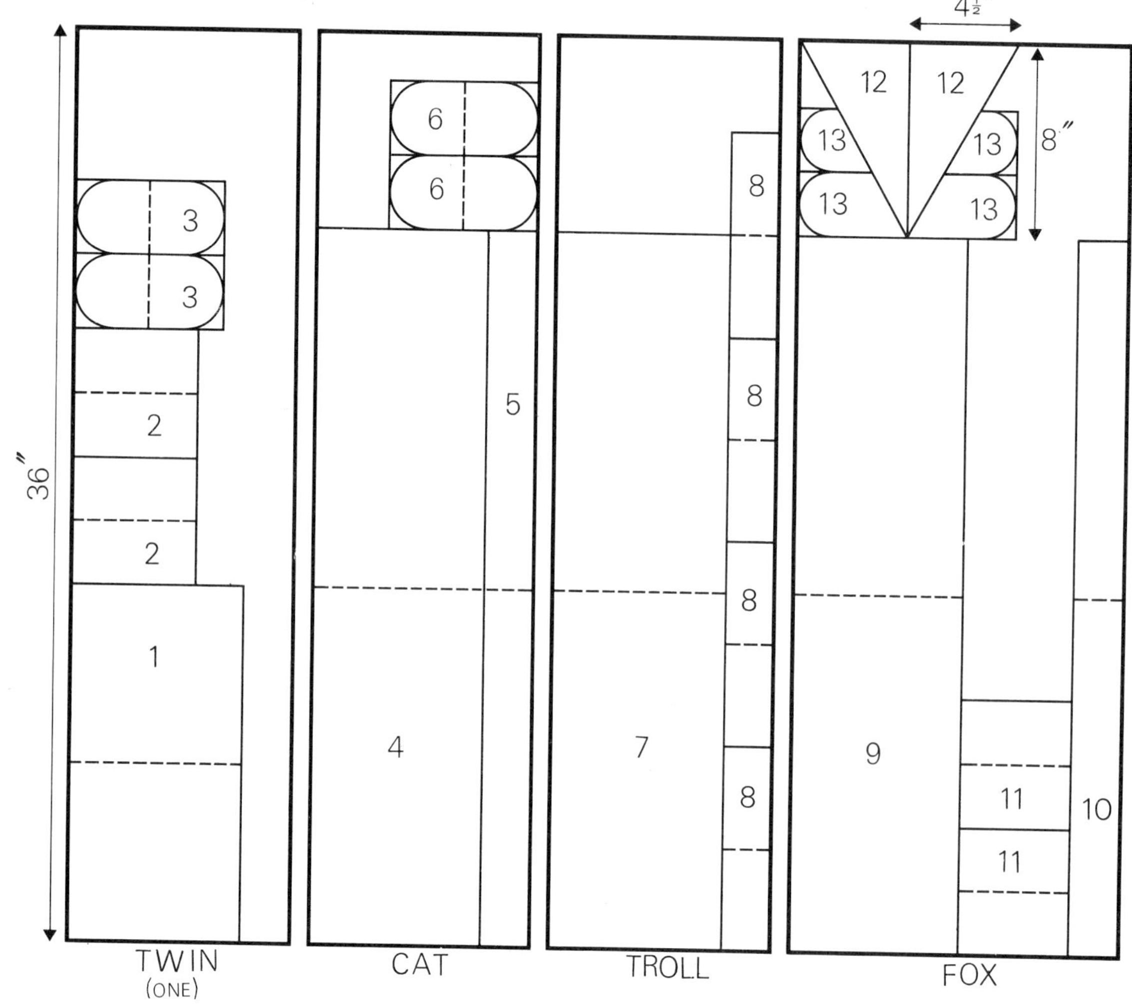

ELLE/TRANSWORLD

Sew on two buttons for eyes and a 3-inch length of string, knotted at each end, for the mouth.

Siamese twins

Make up one double-sized body with four arms and legs as above and decorate each side of body as for separate girl and boy twins.

The cat

Fold the ear pieces double along the dotted line and stitch round, leaving a 1-inch opening. Turn to right side and slipstitch opening to close.

Fold the tail piece double on the dotted pattern line and stitch the two long edges. Turn to the right side.

Fold the body piece double on the dotted pattern line and, setting the ears and tail inside the seam, positioning them as in the photograph, stitch around the three sides leaving a 3-inch opening.

Turn to the right side and stuff. Slipstitch opening to close.

Sew on two buttons for eyes and three 6-inch lengths of string for the whiskers.

The troll

Fold each leg piece along the dotted pattern line and stitch long edges. Turn to right side and stuff.

Cut the body in half along the dotted pattern line, set the four legs into the seams, as in the photograph, and stitch around the sides, leaving a 3-inch opening.

Turn to the right side and stuff. Slipstitch opening to close.

Sew on two buttons for eyes, a length of string for the mouth and two buttons on the body front.

Cut the string into 6-inch lengths. Bind into three bundles and sew to the top body edge —one in the centre and one to either side.

The fox

Match the ear pieces in pairs and stitch around the edges, leaving slanted edge open. Turn to the right side.

Stitch the triangular head pieces together, setting the ears into the slanting seam towards the top, as in the photograph, and leaving a 2-inch opening for turning. Turn to the right side and stuff. Slipstitch opening to close.

Fold the tail strip double along the dotted pattern line and stitch the long edge. Turn to the right side.

Fold the body piece double along the dotted pattern line, set the tail into the seam at the end of the long edge and stitch around the three sides leaving a 2-inch opening. Turn to the right side and stuff. Slipstitch opening to close.

Slipstitch head in place.

Fold the leg pieces along the dotted pattern line and stitch the long edges and one end. Turn to the right side and stuff. Turn in seam allowance on the open edges and slipstitch together. Slipstitch legs to the body, as in the photograph.

Sew on a ball button for the eye and three 6-inch lengths of string, caught together under the nose, for whiskers.

terence the terrible

Terence is a giant felt tortoise about 2 foot long with multi-coloured patchwork scales. The scales are stitched in place with zig-zag machine stitch.

Materials required

$\frac{7}{8}$ yard 72-inch wide green felt
$\frac{3}{8}$ yard 72-inch wide yellow felt
Scraps blue and white felt for eyes
Assorted scraps fabric for scales
Embroidery thread for mouth
Kapok or synthetic wadding for filling

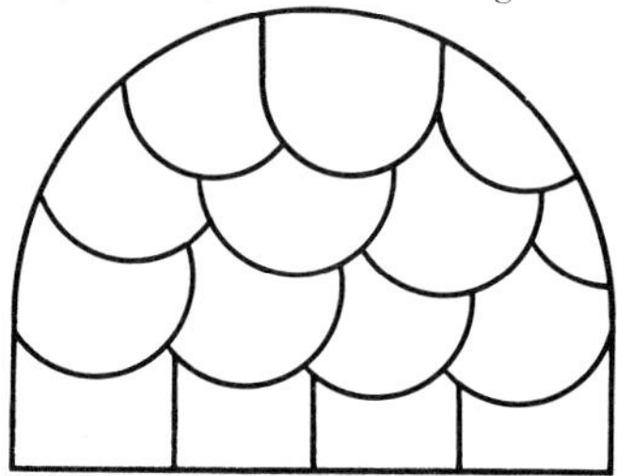

FIG 1

To make pattern

See Know-How.
The pattern pieces you will need are:
1. Underbody (cut 1 on fold); **2.** Body (cut 2); **3.** Head (cut 2); **4.** Foot and tail (cut 10); **5.** Scale (cut about 40).

To cut out

Follow the cutting layouts. The pattern has $\frac{3}{8}$-inch seam allowance.
The underbody (**1**) and body (**2**) are cut from green felt. The head, tail and feet are cut from yellow felt. Cut about 40 scales from assorted scraps of fabric.

Making up

All seams are stitched with right sides together, unless otherwise stated.
Following Figure 1, appliqué the scales to the two body pieces using a zig-zag stitch on the machine. Start at the base of the body and work up.
Arrange the tail and feet pieces in pair and stitch round outer curved edges. Tur to right side and fill lightly. Position fe and tail to right side of body, raw edge level. Tack in place.
Stitch the body pieces together along th curved back edge from A to B.
Position underbody to body and stitch a round, taking tail and feet into seam. Eas underbody to body piece and leave a 4-inc opening along one side.
Turn right side out and stuff firmly. Tur in seam allowance along opening and dra stitch with double thread to close.
Stitch head pieces together leaving straigh neck end open. Turn to right side an embroider mouth in stem stitch. Sew o eyes or stick in place with fabric adhesive Turn in seam allowance at neck edge an tack. Fill head then oversew firmly to body.

72 INCH FABRIC
SELVEDGES

72 INCH FABRIC
SELVEDGES

EACH SQUARE REPRESENTS 1 INCH SQUARE
SEAM ALLOWANCES ARE INCLUDED

2
BODY

A B

5
SCALE

1
UNDERBODY

FOLD

4
FOOT AND TAIL

3
HEAD

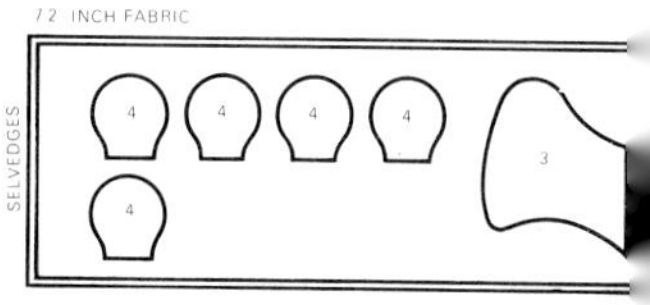

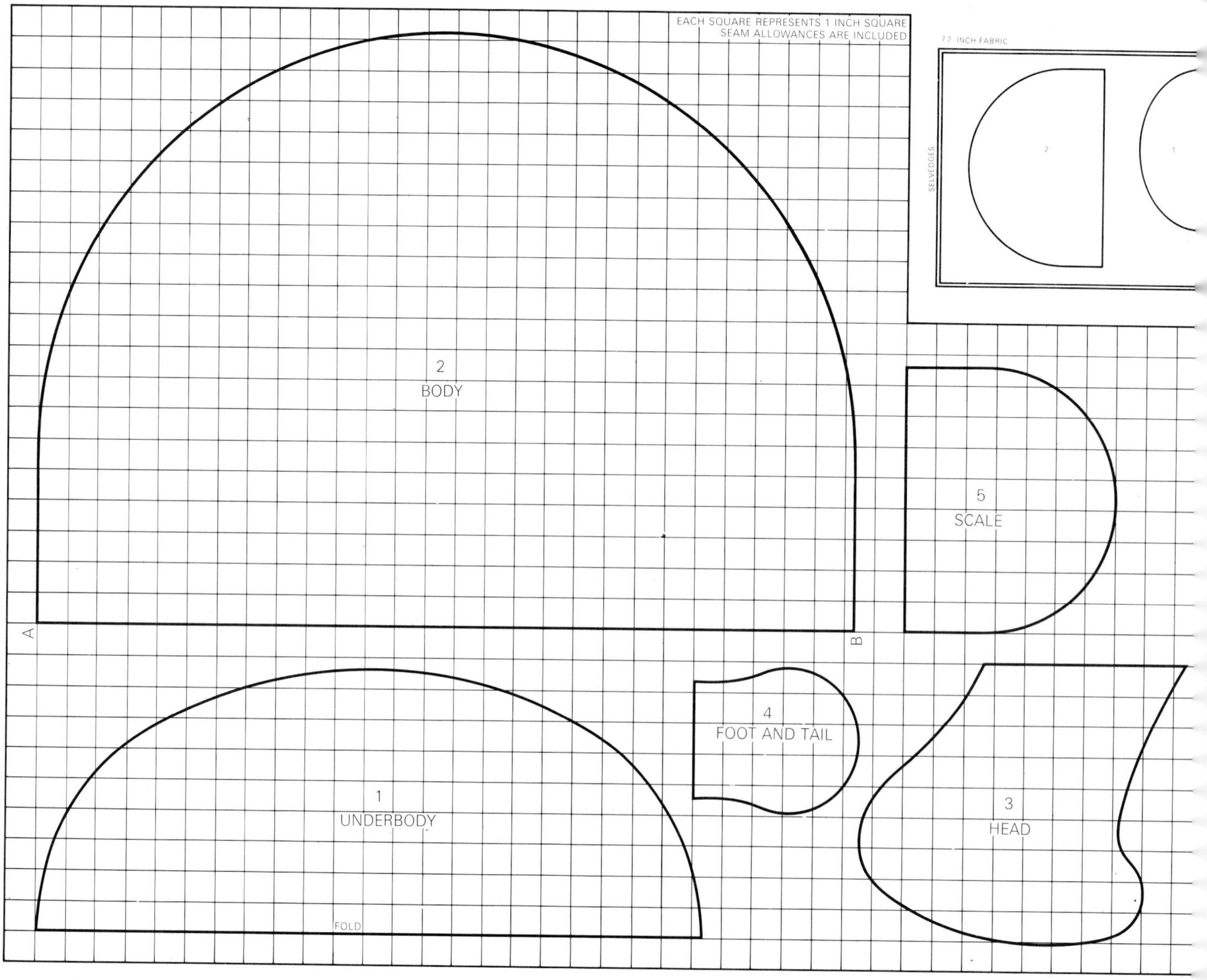

BETA PICTURES

samson the giant snail

Samson the giant snail can be ridden, sat upon, tossed about, and he really does not mind. Made in a jersey fabric, with suede appliqué, he is a firm favourite with children, and makes a super cushion. His finished height is about 25 inches.

Materials required

2 yards 60-inch wide jersey fabric
Suede scraps in assorted shades
Foam pieces for filling shell
Kapok for filling head
Two large 'joggle' eyes
Leather needle for machine
Transparent sticky tape

To make pattern

See Know-How.

The pattern pieces you will need are: **1.** Head (cut 2); **2.** Head gusset (cut 1); **3.** Suede shell patch—large (cut 14); **4.** Suede shell patch—small (cut 40).

To cut out

The pattern includes $\frac{1}{2}$-inch seam allowanc Follow the cutting layout for the jerse fabric.

From jersey fabric cut two $17\frac{1}{2}$-inch wid bias strips for shell, joining to mak up 3-yard length.

Using templates cut out about 14 large she patches (**3**) and 40 small shell patches (4 from suede; work with sharp scissors drawing round templates with ballpoint pen Cut random numbers of pieces in each shad or arrange as you wish.

Making up

All seams are stitched with right sides together, unless otherwise stated. Use a smal zig-zag machine stitch throughout if possibl for more elasticity.

Shell: Join bias strips to make about 3-yar length for shell. Taper each end of the stri to a point.

Using sticky tape to hold in place, positio shell patches along fabric strip, keepin large patches together at one end as show in Figure 1 (these will form outer circle o shell). Arrange small patches in pairs a shown, beginning 2 inches from each edge the central gaps will be covered by successiv layers of shell.

Appliqué patches to shell strip, work on righ side using leather needle in machine and large zig-zag stitch.

With right sides together stitch long sean of shell strip, beginning at tapered en where small patches have been used, thi forms centre of shell. Leave other end oper for filling.

Turn to right side for about 1 yard fron stitched end, this makes filling easier. Begi filling fairly firmly with foam pieces. Continu pulling roll through to right side an filling until the other end is reached. Overse end to close.

Now coil padded roll round to form shell pinning firmly. Beginning in centre an using double thread, firmly stitch coil together so that gaps between the patche are covered by successive layers of shell. Larg patches form outer edge and any remainin gaps will be covered by the head.

Head: Stitch each side of the gusset to th head pieces from A to B, leaving 1-inch gap for horns as indicated. Stitch from A to C leaving BC open for filling. Turn to right sid and fill. Oversew opening together.

For each horn, take piece of suede, about 8 inches by 10 inches, roll up and stitch to secure. Sew horns firmly into head as in the photograph.

Stitch 'joggle' eyes to face.

For eyelids, cut semi-circles of suede, slightl larger than eyes, position and stitch a shown. For nose, take one small shel patch, roll up a bit from narrow end, stitc to secure and sew to face.

Pin head to body and stitch firmly in place positioning neck seam centrally and covering the end of the snail coil. Stitch dow sides of neck so that it tapers into shell and covers any remaining gaps between suede patches.

CHRIS LEWIS

SUEDE SHELL PATCH
— LARGE
SUEDE SHELL PATCH
— SMALL
4
3
A
2
HEAD GUSSET
HORNS
1
HEAD
A
B
C
B
CH SQUARE REPRESENTS 1 INCH SQUARE
EAM ALLOWANCES ARE INCLUDED

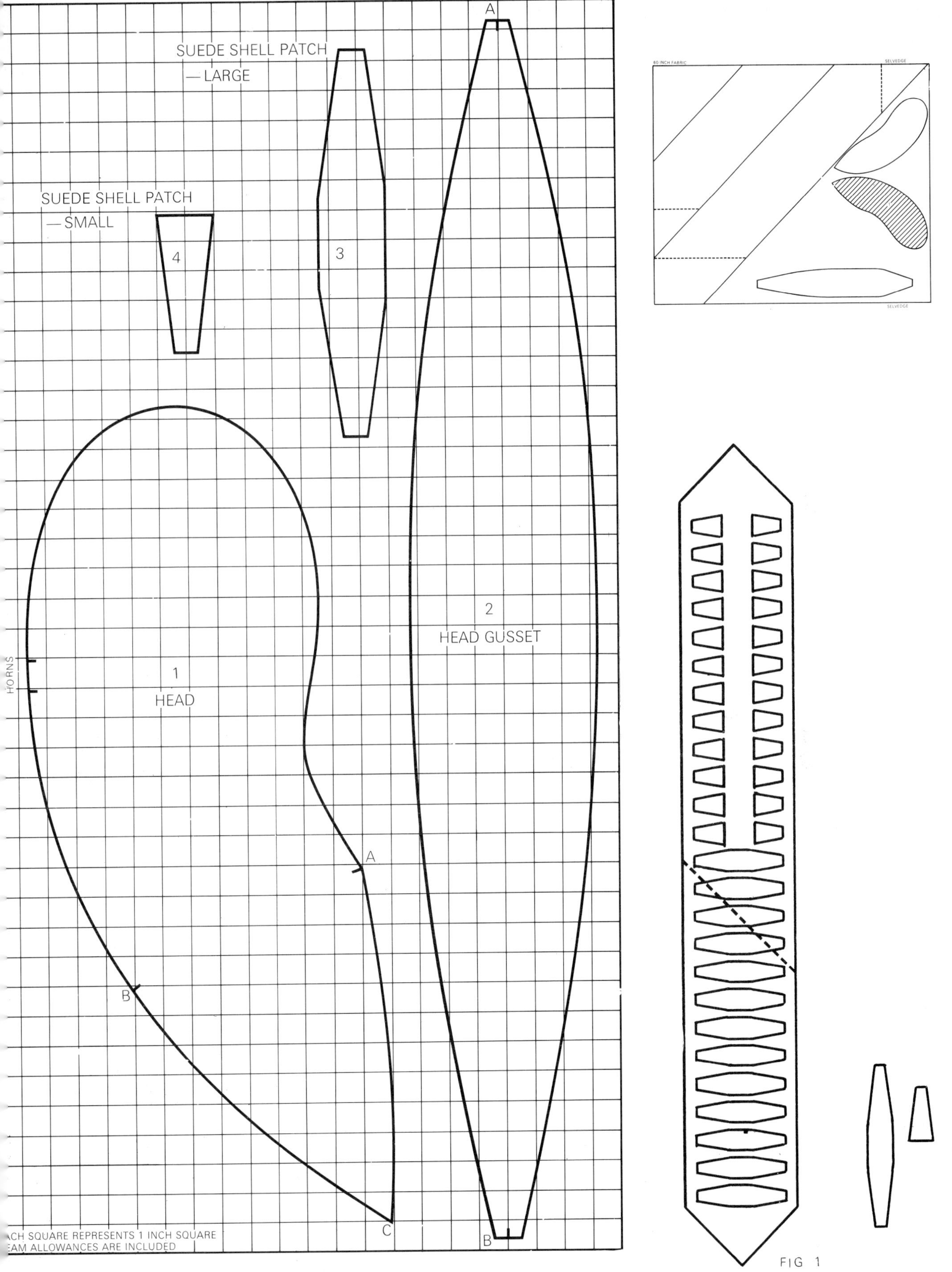

FIG 1

CHRIS LEWIS

marmalade cat and the little white mouse

A satisfied-looking cat with mouse in paw. Marmalade is made from foam sheeting and is about 5 inches high.

Materials required

1-inch thick foam sheeting, 5 inches by 7 inches
9-inch square orange felt
Scraps felt in pink, pale orange and white
Scraps stranded embroidery cotton in pink, green, pale orange and grey
Copydex or other fabric adhesive
Scrap wadding for filling
Stiff paper for pattern
Two pipe cleaners

To make pattern

The pattern pieces you will need are:
1. Cat body (cut 2 in foam); **2.** Cat body covering (cut 1 on fold); **3.** Cat ear (cut 4); **4.** Cat arm (cut 4).
Transfer cat body pattern (**1**) to stiff paper.
No pattern pieces are needed for the mouse.

To cut out

No seam allowances are required.
Cut two cat body pieces from foam. Place pattern on foam and draw round with felt tip pen. Cut out with sharp scissors.
Cut one cat body covering on fold, two outer ears and four arms from orange felt.
Cut two inner ears from pale orange felt. All other cat pieces are cut out as you go.

Making up the mouse

Cut a piece of foam 1 inch by $\frac{1}{2}$ inch and a piece of white felt $1\frac{1}{4}$ inches by 1 inch.
Wrap felt round foam, lower edge level with base. Oversew long edges together, making a stuffed tubular shape. The seam goes to the back of the mouse.
Gather around top edge of felt, drawing up to close. This forms the head.
For feet cut two very small ovals in white felt and stick to foam at base so that they protrude forward.
Cut round of white felt to fit base. Stick in place then oversew all round.
For ears cut $\frac{3}{8}$-inch diameter circles, two in white and two in pink. Stick them together in pairs. Pleat base and stitch to head.
Cut narrow strips white felt for tail and front paws and stitch to mouse.
Embroider prominent pink nose and tiny grey eyes. Make short whiskers from white cotton thread.

Making up the cat

Stick foam body pieces together.
Wrap body covering round foam, base edges level, and oversew edges together down centre back.
Gather up top edge to leave an exposed piece of foam about $\frac{3}{4}$-inch across. Cut a round of orange felt to this shape and oversew in place.
Similarly sew a round of felt to the base.
Stick inner and outer ears together in pai then oversew neatly all round. Stitch t top of head curving base as shown.
Cut two oval eyes from white felt and stic in place. Embroider green pupils in sati stitch.
Stick on pale orange felt nose, embroide pale orange mouth in stem stitch and whit whiskers in long stitches as shown.
Decorate body with irregular strips pal orange felt, slipstitched in place, an lines of pale orange stem stitch.
For tail cut piece orange felt 2 inches b 5 inches. Cut two 5-inch lengths pip cleaner. Roll felt round pipe cleaners, padding with a little wadding. Slipstitch edge down and across each end.
Decorate tail as for body. Stitch firmly t centre back and wrap round body.
Arrange arm pieces in pairs, oversew together, filling with a little wadding. Embroider claws in pale orange straight stitches Sew to body.
Stitch mouse to one of the cat's paws.

pansy piglet

Pansy the flowery pink piglet with the curl tail is made from felt and foam. She is jus $3\frac{1}{2}$ inches high.

Materials required

1-inch thick foam sheeting, 12 inches square
Pale pink felt 12 inches by 24 inches
Scraps felt in grey, rose pink, turquoise, gold, white and two colours green
Scraps stranded embroidery cotton in green white, grey and pink
Pipe cleaner
Stiff paper for pattern
Copydex or other fabric adhesive

To make pattern

See Know-How.
No seam allowances are required.
The pattern pieces you will need are:
1. Body (cut 3); **2.** Ear (cut 4).
Transfer body shape to stiff paper.

To cut out

Cut two ears from pale pink felt and two ears from rose pink. The rest of the fel pieces are cut out as you are making up the pig.
Cut 3 body pieces from foam. To do this place pattern on foam and draw round it. Cut out with scissors. Where possible, place base of leg shapes to straight edge of foam so that the animal has a completely flat base to stand upon.

Making up

Using the adhesive, stick the three foam body pieces together. When dry dab both sides of pig with adhesive and press on to pale pink felt. Allow to dry and trim felt to edge all round.
Following Figure 1, shape the pig by catch-

ng the edges of both felt side body pieces together across the foam with thread lacing. Points AA should be pulled together to measure $1\frac{1}{4}$ inches. Extend the lacing to BB so that width at this point is once more 3 inches. Similarly lace from C to D, making CC $\frac{3}{4}$ inch and DD $1\frac{1}{2}$ inches. Shape from F to E, making FF measure $1\frac{3}{4}$ inches and EE the original 3 inches.

For the gusset cut a strip pale pink felt $15\frac{1}{2}$ inches by $2\frac{1}{2}$ inches. Dab adhesive on all uncovered edges of pig, then, starting at point A, stick gusset right round pig, stabbing in pins to secure while it dries. Trim away overhanging areas of felt.

Using matching thread neatly oversew gusset to side body felt all round, drawing edges tightly together.

Cut piece rose felt for snout and slipstitch in place.

For the trotters stick oblongs of grey felt to bottom of feet, trimming to shape. Cut $\frac{3}{4}$-inch strips grey felt long enough to go round both pairs of legs and sew to oblong as in the picture.

Stick rose ear to pink ear. Oversew all round.

To shape the ear at base, with inner rose pink uppermost bring points G to meet as you can see on the photograph. Then catch points together with thread. Stitch base of ear to pig, parallel to and about $\frac{5}{8}$ inch in from gusset seam. Arrange ear at good angle and catch the back edge down to gusset seam to hold in this position.

For tail cut piece pale pink felt $\frac{3}{4}$ inch by $3\frac{1}{2}$ inches. Fold pipe cleaner in half. Fold felt over it and oversew edges. Sew end of tail securely to back of pig then curl tail in a spiral.

Make up eyes in grey and white felt circles as in picture and slipstitch in place. Add grey eyelashes and white pupils.

Embroider nostrils in pink and grey stem stitch circles.

Embroider pink mouth with several strands of pink embroidery thread held down by couching.

Embroider separating line for back and front legs with short line of grey stitches.

Cut tiny flowers and leaves from scraps of felt in remaining colours. Stick to pig adding straight stitches in green and white french knots.

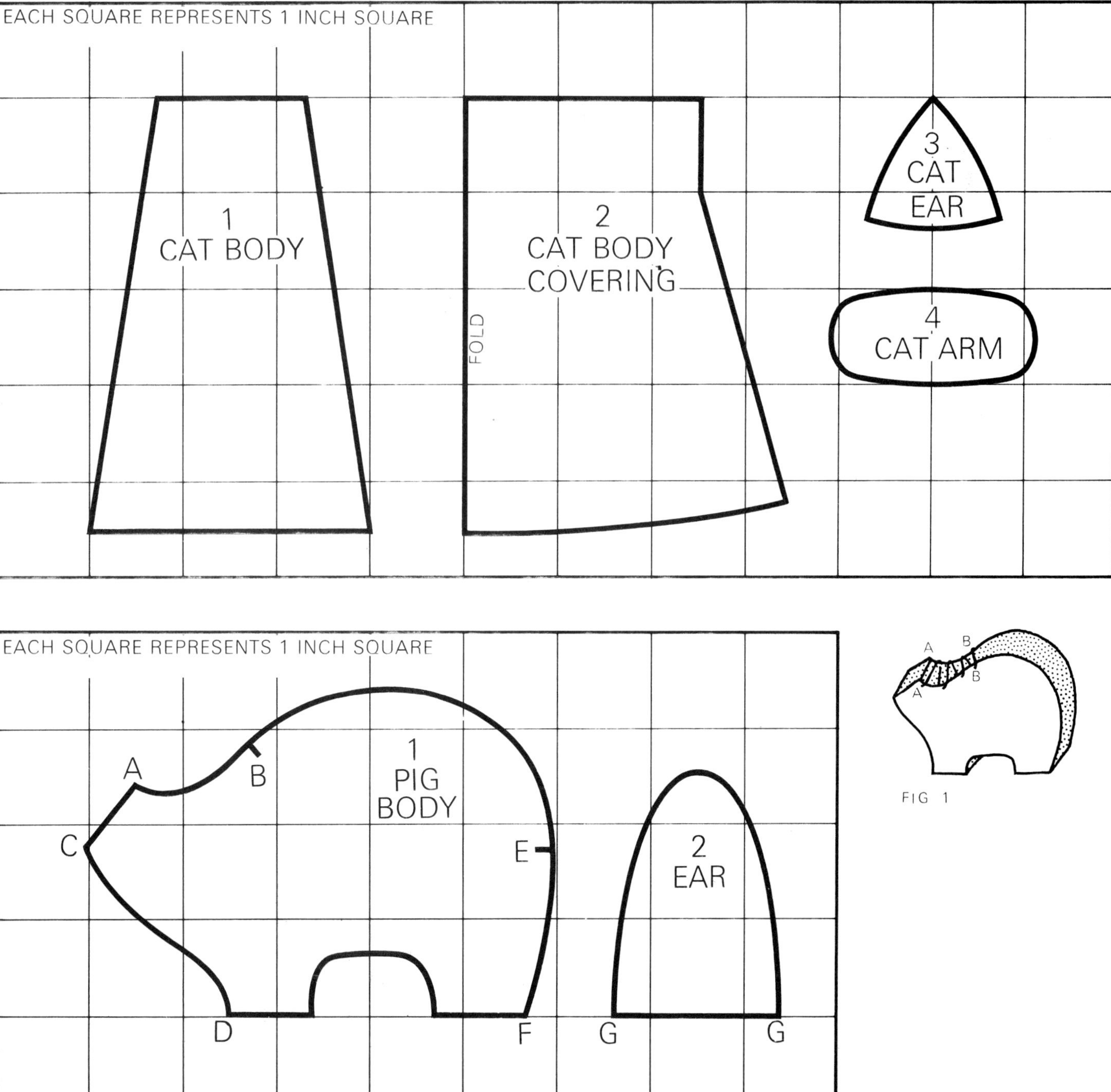

FIG 1

hadrian the hippo

Hadrian is a 3-foot long hippopotamus of great charm. A solid and dependable playmate, he is cheap and simple to make and a most unusual addition to your children's room.

Materials required

2 yards of 36-inch wide hessian or sacking
Red felt 12 inches by 24 inches
Scraps of felt in black and white for eyes
Wood wool for filling
Fabric adhesive

To make pattern

See Know-How.

The pattern pieces you will need are: **1.** Ear (cut 4); **2.** Side (cut 2); **3.** Inner leg (cut 4); **4.** Tail (cut 1); **5.** Head gusset (cut 1); **6.** Snout (cut 1); **7.** Stomach (cut 1); **8.** Sole (cut 4).

To cut out

Follow the cutting layouts. The pattern has $\frac{1}{2}$-inch seam allowance included.

From the red felt cut two ear pieces (**1**) and four sole pieces (**8**).

Making up

All seams are stitched with right sides together unless otherwise stated. Take $\frac{1}{2}$-inch seams throughout.

Stitch felt and hessian ear pieces together in pairs leaving straight edge open. Turn to right side.

Bring the edges of the ear at A to meet at centre point B with the red inside as in the photograph, and tack. Set each ear, facing forward, into the head dart on each side piece. Stitch the darts.

Stitch the inner leg pieces to the legs on the side pieces leaving the top and bottom edges open. Turn to right side.

Fold the tail in half lengthways and stitch edges together, leaving one short end open. Turn to right side and fill lightly.

Stitch the stomach piece to the snout and the snout piece to the head gusset, matching notches throughout.

Stitch the sides of the snout piece to the side pieces between C and D.

Stitch the head gusset to the side pieces along both edges to meet at the pointed end.

Stitch the stomach piece to the side pieces,

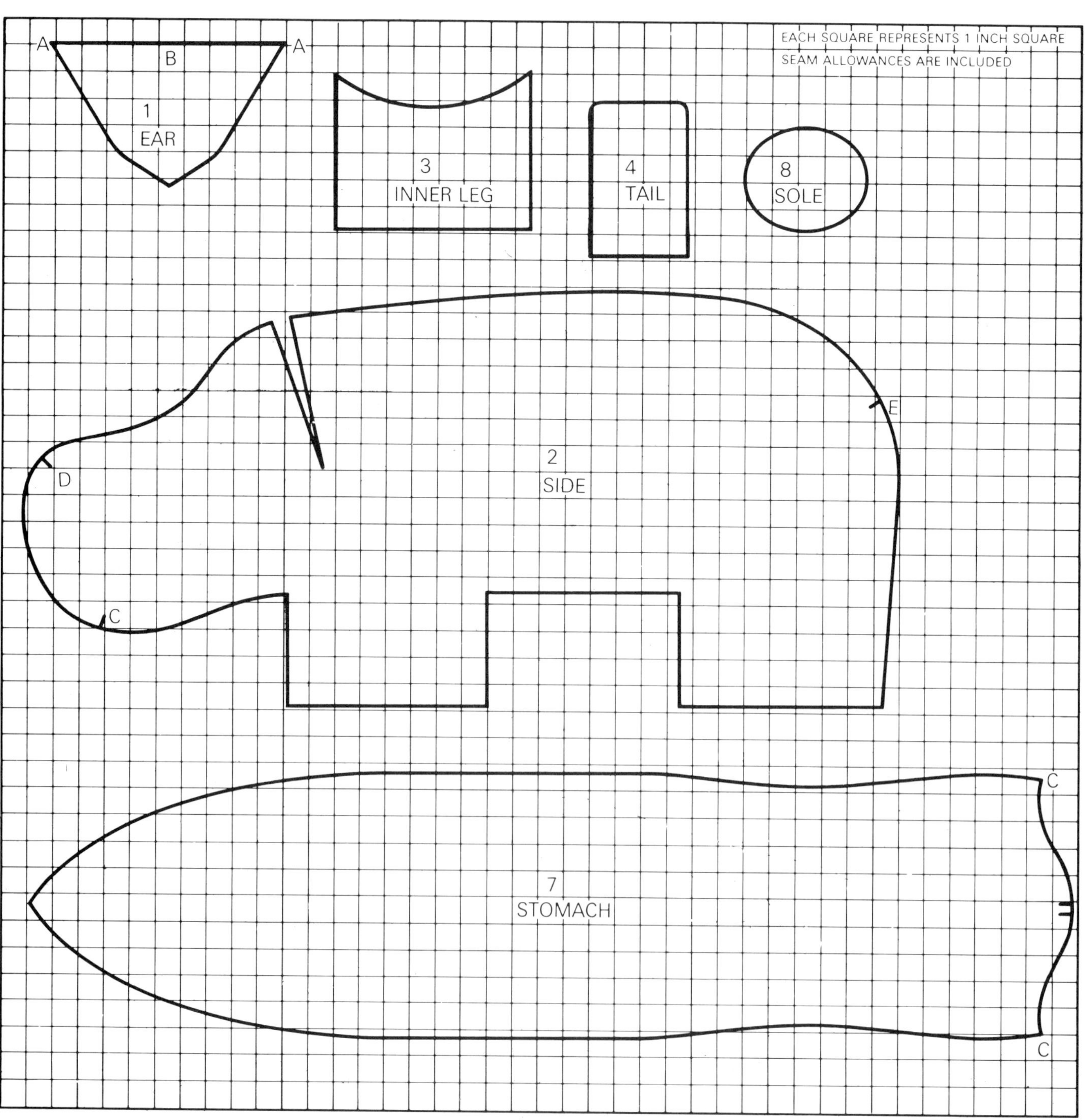

stitching round the inside of the leg pieces and leaving a 6-inch opening between the legs on one side for stuffing.

Then, setting the tail in to the seam at E, stitch the side pieces together along the back seam to the beginning of the head piece.

Turn the hippo to the right side and stuff firmly with wood wool. Close the open seam by hand, using ladder stitch.

Stuff each leg really firmly through its open end and slipstitch a sole piece over the end of each leg, adding extra wood wool as necessary.

Cut out black and white felt eye pieces and stick in position as in the photograph.

Cut two strips of red felt $\frac{1}{2}$ inch by 4 inches, and roll up tightly to make a $\frac{1}{2}$-inch scroll. Fix scroll with adhesive and stitch one on either side of snout as in photograph.

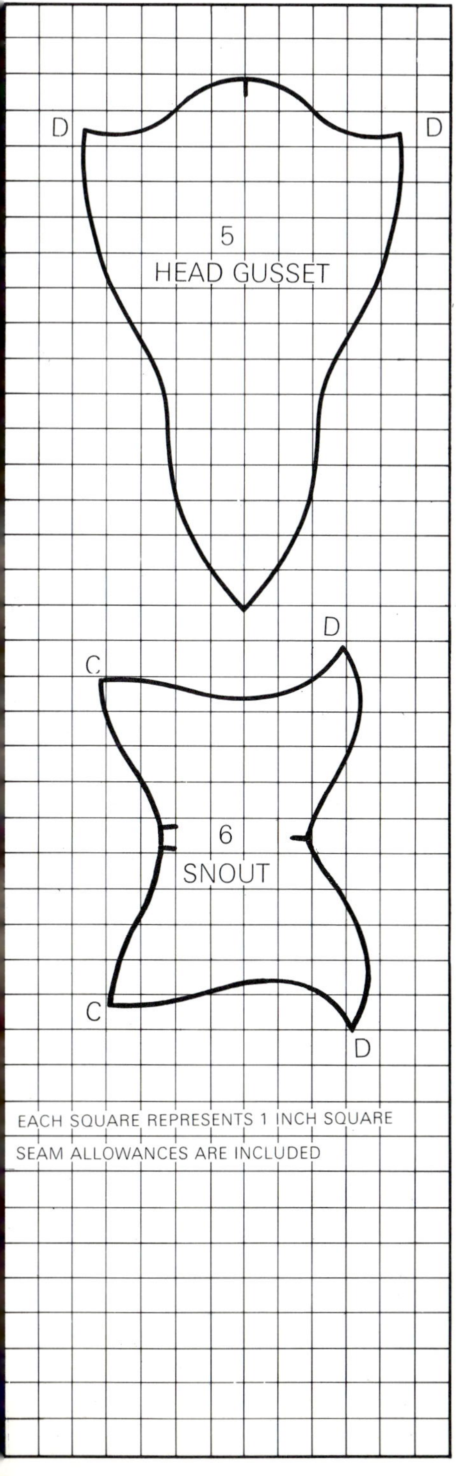

BETA PICTURES

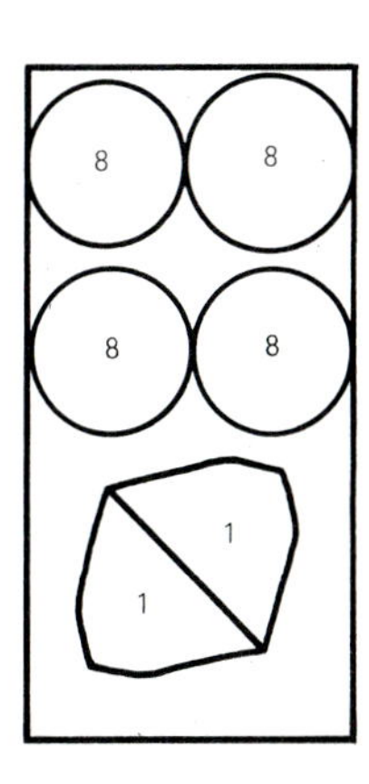

josephine the giraffe

Josephine is a giraffe with a special look in her eye. Made in cotton, with a furry mane and huge eyes, she stands just over one foot high. The giraffe on the cover is an 18-inch version—turn to the end of the instructions for details.

Small giraffe

Materials required

$\frac{1}{2}$ yard 36-inch wide cotton fabric
Scrap of plain fabric for ears
12 inches of 1-inch wide fur trimming
Scraps of felt in black, white and brown
Kapok for filling

To make pattern

See Know-How.
The pattern pieces you will need are:
1. Body (cut 2); **2.** Gusset (cut 2); **3.** Tail (cut 1); **4.** Ear (cut 4); **5. a, b, c.** Eye (cut 2 of each).

To cut out

Follow the cutting layout. The pattern includes a $\frac{1}{4}$-inch seam allowance.
Also cut two ear pieces (**4**) from plain fabric.
From felt cut the eye pieces (**5**), cutting **5a** twice in white, **5b** twice in black and **5c** twice in brown. From the fur strip cut $1\frac{1}{2}$ inches for the tail, the rest being the mane.

Making up

All seams are stitched right sides together, unless otherwise stated.
On each gusset piece stitch the darts as indicated on the pattern piece.
Stitch the gusset pieces together from B to C. Match the gusset to the body pieces and stitch to each side from B through D, E, F, G to C. Stitch the body pieces together from B through A to O.
Fold the mane strip in half lengthways, right side out, and set into the seam between the body pieces with the fur inside and raw edges together. Tack and stitch from O to M.
Stitch from N to C leaving an opening from M to N. Snip the curved seam allowances between the legs and under the chin. Turn to the right side and stuff firmly. Close the opening with ladder stitch.
Fold the tail piece in half lengthways and stitch the long edges together. Roll up the small piece of fur and insert inside one end of the tail. Stitch firmly. Turn the tail to the right side and fill lightly. Slipstitch the open end of the tail in position at C.
Stitch plain and patterned ear pieces together in pairs leaving short side open. Turn to the right side. Turn in the seam allowance on the raw edges and tack the edges together. Stitch an ear in position on either side of the head as marked on the pattern, the plain side of the ear facing forward.

CHRIS LEWIS

Assemble the black and white eye pieces (**5a** and **b**) and sew on either side of the head, as indicated on the pattern. Around the upper curve of the eye slipstitch the plain edge of the brown eye piece, so that the 'lid' curves out over the eye.
To make the 'mouth' push the material at the end of the nose in to form a horizontal pleat. Pull edges together with invisible stitches to make the lips.

arge giraffe

he giraffe on the cover is $1\frac{1}{2}$ times the size f the original. The Know-How section the beginning shows how to enlarge a raph pattern. This giraffe also differs on a w details—he has a looped woollen mane, uede ears and eyelids.

o make the mane

ou will need: $\frac{1}{2}$ ounce of double knitting wool; a strip of stiff paper 14 inches by 3 inches.

To make: Fold the paper lengthways. Fasten the wool at one end and bind closely around the folded paper all along its length. Fasten the end and cut the wool.

Machine stitch, $\frac{1}{4}$-inch in from the edge, along the strip through wool and paper. Carefully tear away the paper base. Cut 2 inches off mane for the tail tassel.

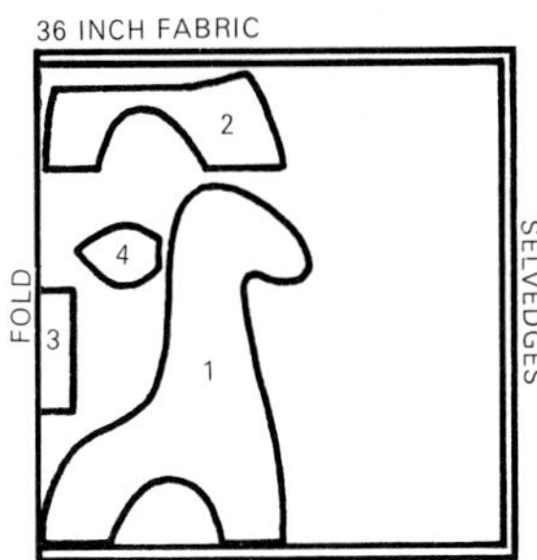

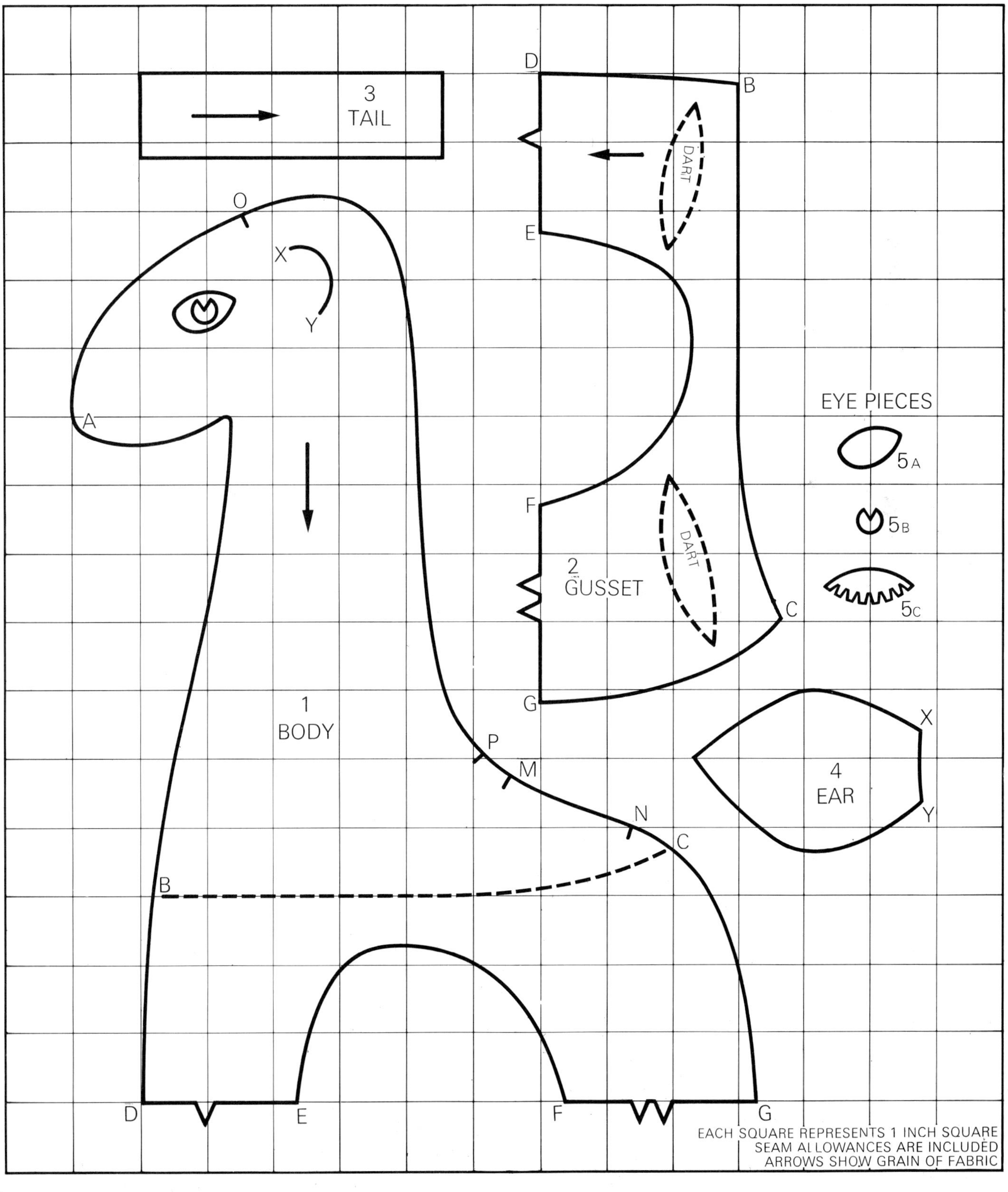

3 TAIL

1 BODY

2 GUSSET

DART

EYE PIECES

5A

5B

5C

4 EAR

EACH SQUARE REPRESENTS 1 INCH SQUARE
SEAM ALLOWANCES ARE INCLUDED
ARROWS SHOW GRAIN OF FABRIC

wol the performing owl

CHRIS LEWIS

An unusual performing owl to amuse young and old alike. He is made from scraps of felt, a piece of wood dowelling and a curtain ring, with an internal mechanism that is ingenious but simple.
When the ring is pulled he flaps his wings. The overall height, including the striped pole, is 12 inches.

Materials required
7-inch square of apricot brushed acrylic fabric
Strip of orange felt 1 inch by 12 inches
Scraps of felt in orange, yellow and black
7-inch square of brown felt
One pipe cleaner
Two small black beads
One ping-pong ball
Lead dress weight approximately 1-inch in diameter
One 1-inch diameter curtain ring
Embroidery thread and button thread in same brown as the felt
12 inches of $\frac{1}{4}$-inch diameter dowelling
6-inch square of thick cardboard
Copydex or other fabric adhesive

To make pattern
See Know-How.
The pattern pieces you will need are:
1. Body (cut 1); **2.** Back body covering (cut 1); **3.** Top wing (cut 2); **4.** Under-wing (cut 2); **5.** Foot (cut 2); **6.** Beak (cut 1); **7.** Base (cut 1).

To cut out
Cut body (**1**), base (**7**) and two under-wings (**4**) from apricot fabric.
Cut back body covering (**2**) and two top wing pieces (**3**) from brown felt.
The feet (**5**) and beak (**6**) are cut from black felt.
For the eyes cut two $\frac{1}{4}$-inch diameter circles in black felt, two $\frac{1}{2}$-inch circles in orange and two $\frac{5}{8}$-inch circles in yellow.
From cardboard cut four wing pieces (**3**) using top wing pattern and two circles—one $1\frac{1}{2}$ inches and one 2 inches in diameter.
Cut a strip yellow felt 16 inches by $\frac{1}{4}$ inch, joining if necessary to make up required length.

Making up
Fold the strip of orange felt in half lengthways and oversew the edges together along the length and one end. Slip this felt tube over the dowel and close the other end.
Using a scissor point pierce a hole in the ping-pong ball and push in the covered dowel as far as it will go. Cover the join with adhesive and allow to dry. Decorate with yellow strip wound round pole as shown. This can be slipstitched in place or stuck down if preferred.
Pierce a hole in the centre of the $1\frac{1}{2}$-inch diameter circle of card to let in the covered dowel. Push the card up the dowel to $\frac{1}{2}$ inch below the ping-pong ball. Apply adhesive and allow to dry.
Wind thick thread several times around the dowel just below the card. Tie firmly and clip ends.
Using a back stitch sew the sloping edges of the body piece together from A to B, right sides facing. Turn to right side.
Run a gathering thread around the shorter (top) edge and draw it up firmly. Oversew lower edge to prevent fraying. Apply a little adhesive to the top of the ping-pong ball and slip the body piece over it, so that the gathering is stuck to the top of the ball.
Run a double running thread around the body between ping-pong ball and card and draw in a little to form a neck. Secure thread firmly.
Working on back covering catch C to D with two or three oversewing stitches, on either side of head to form 'ears'.
Apply adhesive to top of head and back, taking body seam as centre back. Fit body covering over head as in photograph, and secure to either side at points E and F with several small oversewing stitches. Applying more adhesive, stick down edges of body covering to body and leaving tail free.
For each wing, stick two cardboard wing shapes together, fixing a $\frac{1}{4}$ dress weight between them at the point indicated on the pattern. When dry, stick a cardboard shape to the wrong side of each under wing piece (**4**), leaving a $\frac{1}{4}$-inch seam allowance all round.
Run a gathering thread all round edge. Draw up thread tightly to fit material snugly over cardboard base and secure thread.
Stick a brown felt wing piece (**3**) over the unfinished top side of each wing, matching the edges. Finish wing edges with decorative overcasting in brown embroidery thread, as in photograph.
Firmly slipstitch each wing to the body covering sewing the straight edge of the wing horizontally $\frac{1}{4}$ inch below the neck (E), with the outward curved edge of the wing facing forward. The stitching, while firm, should allow the wings to move freely.
Cut a length of button thread about 12 inches long. Using a darning needle, sew one end of the thread very firmly to the wing tip (G) and secure. Push the needle through the body as shown in Figure 1 and down through cardboard disc. Attach thread to the other wing in the same way.
The space between the ping-pong ball and the cardboard disc may be padded with a little wadding.
Cover the 2-inch cardboard disc with the fabric base piece, drawing up the edges with a gathering thread as for the wings.
With a point of the scissors make a hole in the centre to let in the dowel and pierce a hole on either side for each thread at X.
With the wrong side uppermost, push the base up the dowelling until it is level with the lower body edge. On either side thread the button thread through the corresponding hole in the base and secure the two threads temporarily to the dowel.
Overcast the lower body edge to the edge of the base, stitching the two black felt feet into the seam at the front, $\frac{1}{4}$ inch apart.
Work a few fly stitches in brown thread on the body front to represent feathers.
Using embroidery thread buttonhole stitch closely around the curtain ring. Sew the two threads from the wings very firmly to opposite sides of the ring, making them equal in length.
To make the beak cut 1 inch of pipe cleaner and bend double. Cover this with the black felt beak piece and oversew the long edges together. Stitch the wide end firmly to the centre of the face just under the point of the body covering. Stick this point down over the top of the beak.
Make up eyes as shown, gluing felt circles on top of each other. Stitch a little black bead in the centre with white thread. Stick a whole eye on either side of the beak.

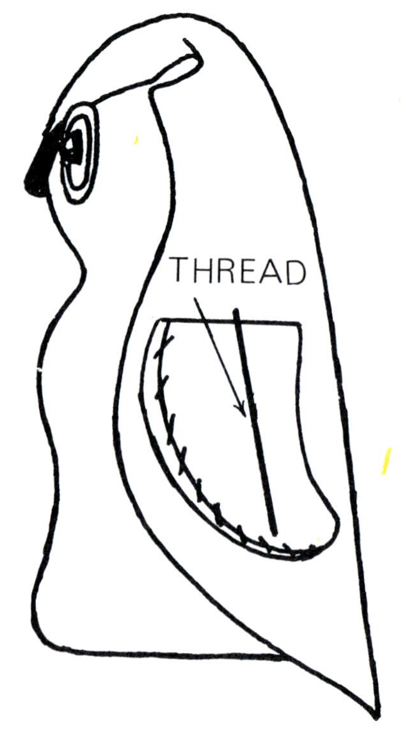

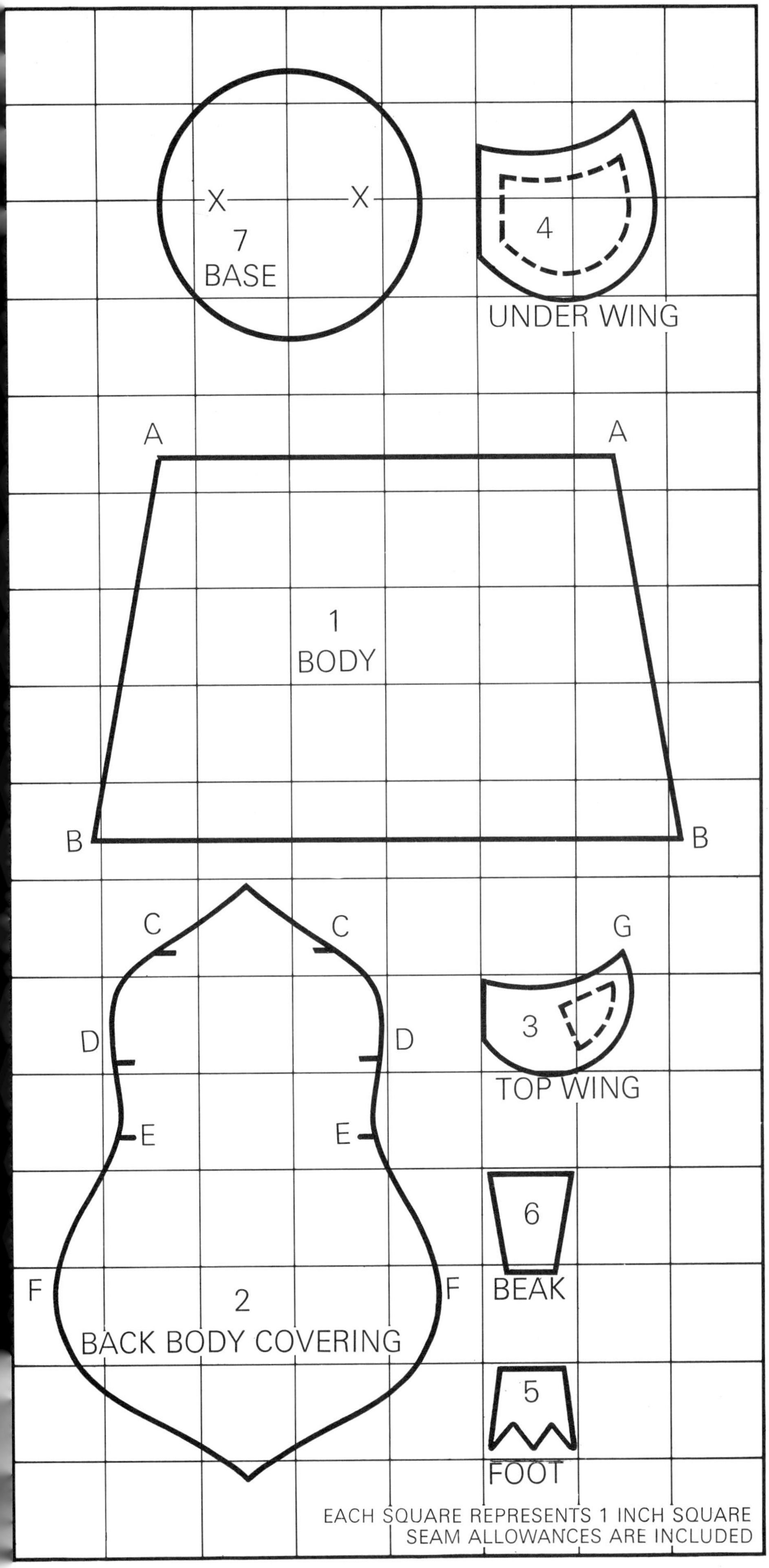

7
BASE

4
UNDER WING

A A

1
BODY

B B

C C
G

D D
3
TOP WING

E E

6
BEAK

F F
2
BACK BODY COVERING

5
FOOT

EACH SQUARE REPRESENTS 1 INCH SQUARE
SEAM ALLOWANCES ARE INCLUDED

CAMERA PRESS

charlie the chimp

his mischievous chimpanzee is made from orduroy and felt and is about 14 inches om head to toe—just the toy for a young ild to drag about the house. Alternatively ou could make him twice the size for a ecorative cushion.

laterials required

yard 36-inch wide corduroy
iece contrasting felt 12 inches square
oam pieces for filling
rown embroidery thread
crap brown wool for the face

'o make pattern

ee Know-How.
'he pattern pieces you will need are:
. Ear (cut 4); **2.** Foot (cut 8).

'o cut out

ollow the cutting layouts. The pattern has -inch seam allowance included where ecessary.

'rom corduroy cut: Two ear pieces (**1**); wo head pieces each $6\frac{3}{4}$ inches by $5\frac{3}{4}$ inches vith the shorter edge running along the tripes; four front leg pieces $5\frac{3}{4}$ inches by inches; four hind leg pieces $11\frac{3}{4}$ inches by inches.

'rom felt cut: eight foot pieces (**2**); two ear ieces; a 4-inch diameter circle for muzzle; wo $2\frac{1}{2}$-inch diameter circles for eyes.

Making up

All seams are stitched with right sides acing and $\frac{3}{8}$ inch seams unless otherwise tated.

)n one head piece stitch on the felt eyes and then the muzzle, using blanket stitch and rown embroidery thread—the $6\frac{3}{4}$-inch ength goes across the head. Using brown vool embroider the mouth in stem stitch nd the pupils in satin stitch.

Arrange foot pieces in pairs, wrong sides ogether. Stitch together leaving top straight dge open. Turn to right side.

Arrange leg pieces in pairs. Stitch together down each long side, turn to right side.

'lace a foot piece at the end of each leg nd blanket stitch in position using brown mbroidery thread. Fill legs lightly.

'lace felt ear pieces to corduroy ear pieces and stitch round curved edge. Turn to right ide.

'osition the legs and ears to the right side of the face with their raw edges level with aw edges of face. Tack in place in seam llowance.

'lace head pieces together, wrong sides acing, and stitch, leaving the piece between he two front legs open and catching legs and ears into the seam. Turn right side out and fill fairly loosely. Turn in seam allowance along opening and slipstitch to close.

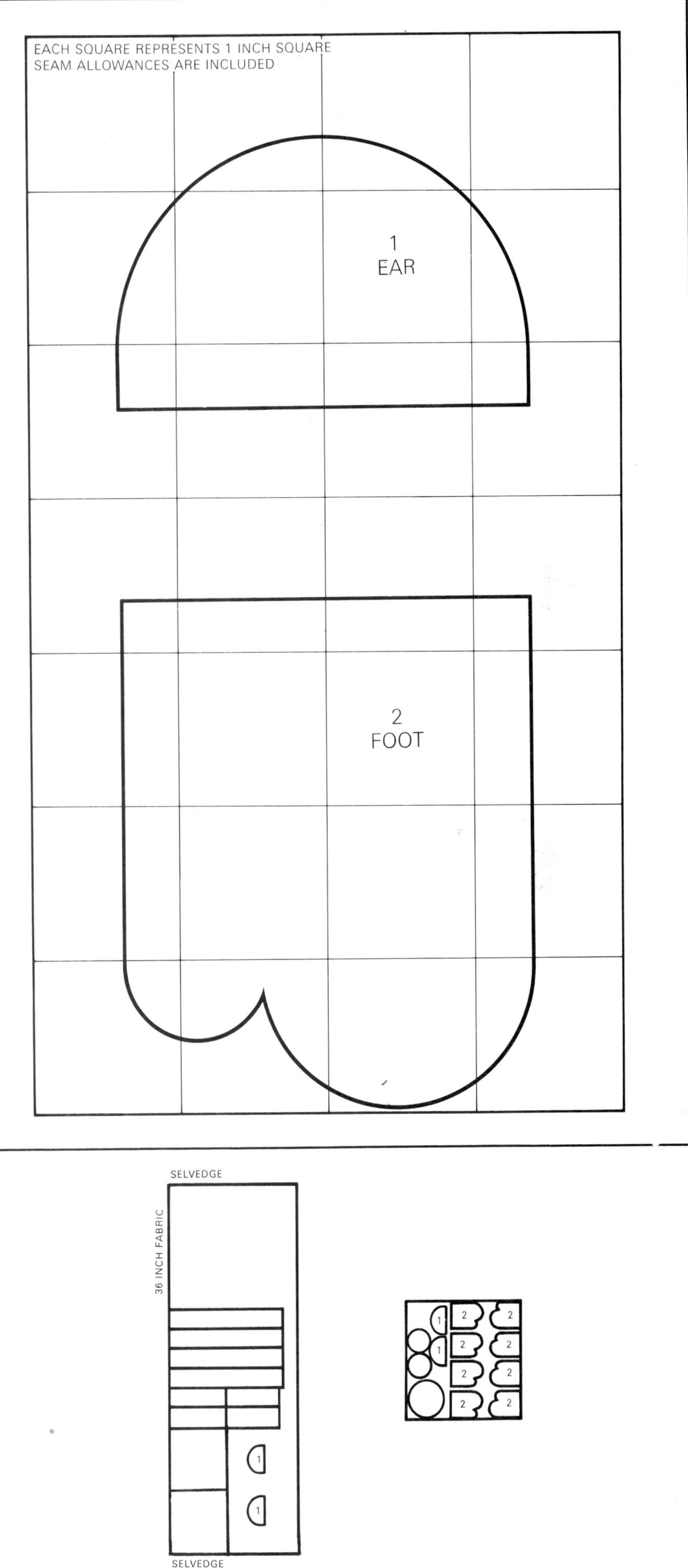

peppermint the polar bear

Peppermint the baby polar is 10 inches long and very life-like. Because he is walking the left and right sides of the body are cut from different pattern pieces.

Materials required

$\frac{3}{8}$ yard 48 or 52-inch wide white fur fabric
9-inch square white felt
Scraps of brown felt
Bodkin
24 inches string
2 glass eyes on wire
Kapok or synthetic wadding for filling
Strong matching thread

To make pattern

See Know-How.

The pattern pieces you will need are: **1.** Head/body right side (cut 1); **2.** Head/body left side (cut 1); **3.** Under body right side (cut 1); **4.** Underbody left side (cut 1); **5.** Head gusset (cut 1); **6.** Foot pad (cut 4); **7.** Ear (cut 4); **8.** Nose piece (cut 1); **9.** Eye piece (cut 2).

To cut out

The pattern has $\frac{1}{4}$-inch seam allowance included.
Follow the fur fabric cutting layout. In white felt cut two ears and four foot pads.
In brown felt cut one nose and two eye-pieces.

Making up

All seams are back stitched with right sides together, taking $\frac{1}{4}$-inch seams, unless otherwise stated.
Make two darts on both left and right underbody pieces as indicated by dotted lines. Then sew underbody pieces together from X to Y.
Sew right underbody to right head/body (**1** and **3**) from X to C, D to E and F to Y. Sew a white foot pad into each of the openings CD and EF.
Sew left underbody to left head/body and insert foot pads similarly.
Stitch head together from X to A. Position head gusset between head pieces and sew both sides from A to B.
Sew back from B to S and T to Y, leaving ST open for filling.
Turn right side out and stuff firmly. Close the opening.
With strong thread and a large needle put several stitches right through the bear's body in the place marked with a star. This gives him a good shape.
Eyes: Cut through the middle of the wire which joins the eyes together. Place a brown felt eye piece on to the wire at the back of each eye. With pliers bend the wire round into a loop.
Cut the length of string in half and tie the centre of one piece to one of the eye loops.
Thread string through a bodkin and push it through the eye position on the bear and out at the ear position. Pull the string

Chris Lewis

hrough and tie off securely.
Repeat with other eye.
Place felt and fur fabric ear pieces together in pairs, right sides together. Sew round outer curved edge. Turn to right side. Slipstitch raw edges together, gather base slightly and sew ears to bear.
Sew darts on the nose piece as indicated by the dotted lines. Fill nose then slipstitch in place.

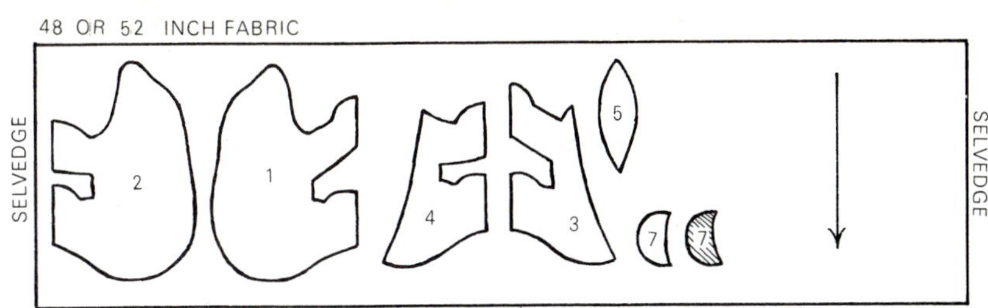

EACH SQUARE REPRESENTS 1 INCH SQUARE
SEAM ALLOWANCES ARE INCLUDED

2
HEAD/BODY LEFT SIDE
A B S T Y X

1
HEAD/BODY RIGHT SIDE
T S B Y A X F E D C

9
EYE PIECE

8
NOSE PIECE

7
EAR

5
HEAD GUSSET
A B

6
FOOT PAD

4
UNDERBODY LEFT SIDE
Y X

3
UNDERBODY RIGHT SIDE
Y X C D E F

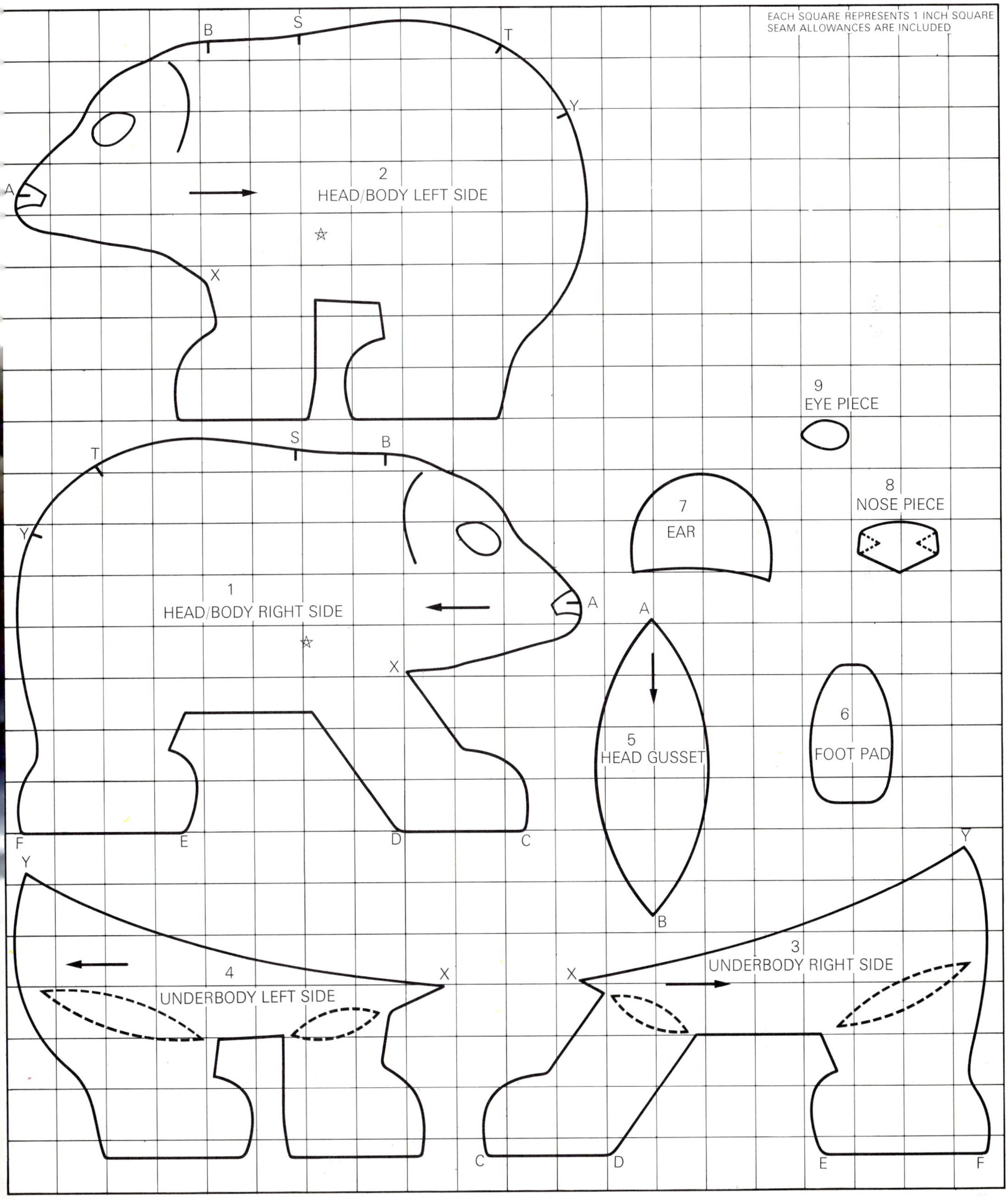

CAMERA PRESS

nellie the elephant

A 9-inch high foam-filled elephant with a ball. The ball pattern can easily be enlarged to any size by adding an equal amount to each side of the pattern.

Materials required

$\frac{1}{2}$ yard 36-inch wide fabric
Foam sheeting 16 inches by 10 inches, 2 inches thick
$\frac{1}{2}$ yard fancy braid for toes
7-inch square felt for ears
Scraps of felt for eyes, tusks and toenails
Scraps of wool for eyelashes
Matching embroidery thread
$\frac{1}{4}$ yard cord for tail
Copydex or other fabric adhesive
Assorted scraps fabric, braid, fringing, for harness and head gear

To make pattern

See Know-How.
The pattern pieces you will need are:
1. Body; **2.** Ear.
The pattern does not include seam allowance, and should be drawn up without.

To cut out

Position the pattern on the foam sheeting and draw round it, using a ball point pen. Cut out with a sharp knife or scissors.
From fabric cut out two body pieces, adding $\frac{1}{2}$ inch all round for seams. Also cut a fabric inset 3 inches wide and long enough to go all round the elephant (about 60 inches) joining strips to make up the required length.
Cut four ears from felt—no seam allowance is necessary.
Cut out eyes, tusks and toenails as in the picture.

Making up

Turn in $\frac{3}{8}$-inch seam allowance all round both body pieces and long edges of inset pieces. Tack.
Sew inset to one body piece all round using a shallow blanket stitch and embroidery thread on the right side.
Place over foam elephant, position other side of body to inset over the foam and sew in place similarly.
Sew darts in each ear piece, making sure you have two top sides and two for underneath. Place together in pairs, wrong sides together, and topstitch all round. Sew in place to each side of elephant.
Using fabric adhesive stick braid to outer sides of each foot and stick felt toenails over the braid.
Cut tail cord to required length. Unravel one end slightly and knot, sew other end to back of elephant.
Stick eyes in place to each side of head and sew on short woollen eyelashes above each eye as shown.
Make up harness and headgear as elaborately as you wish, or leave off altogether.

ball

Materials required

Assorted scraps felt or fur fabric for ball
Washable wadding or kapok for filling

To make pattern

See Know-How.
You will need the following pattern piece:
3. Ball (cut 12).

To cut out

From assorted scraps felt or fur fabric cut out 12 ball pieces. $\frac{1}{4}$-inch seam allowance has been included.

Making up

On all ball pieces turn under seam allowance and tack. The seams of the ball are sewn by placing two straight sides level, right sides together, and then oversewing with a small, but very firm, stitch through the folds.
Taking one of the pieces sew a separate piece to each of its sides, so using up six of the pentagons. Then sew the outer ones to each other at adjacent sides, thus forming a cup Do the same with remaining six. Sew the two cups together, leaving one side open. Turn to right side and fill firmly. Ladder stitch opening to close.

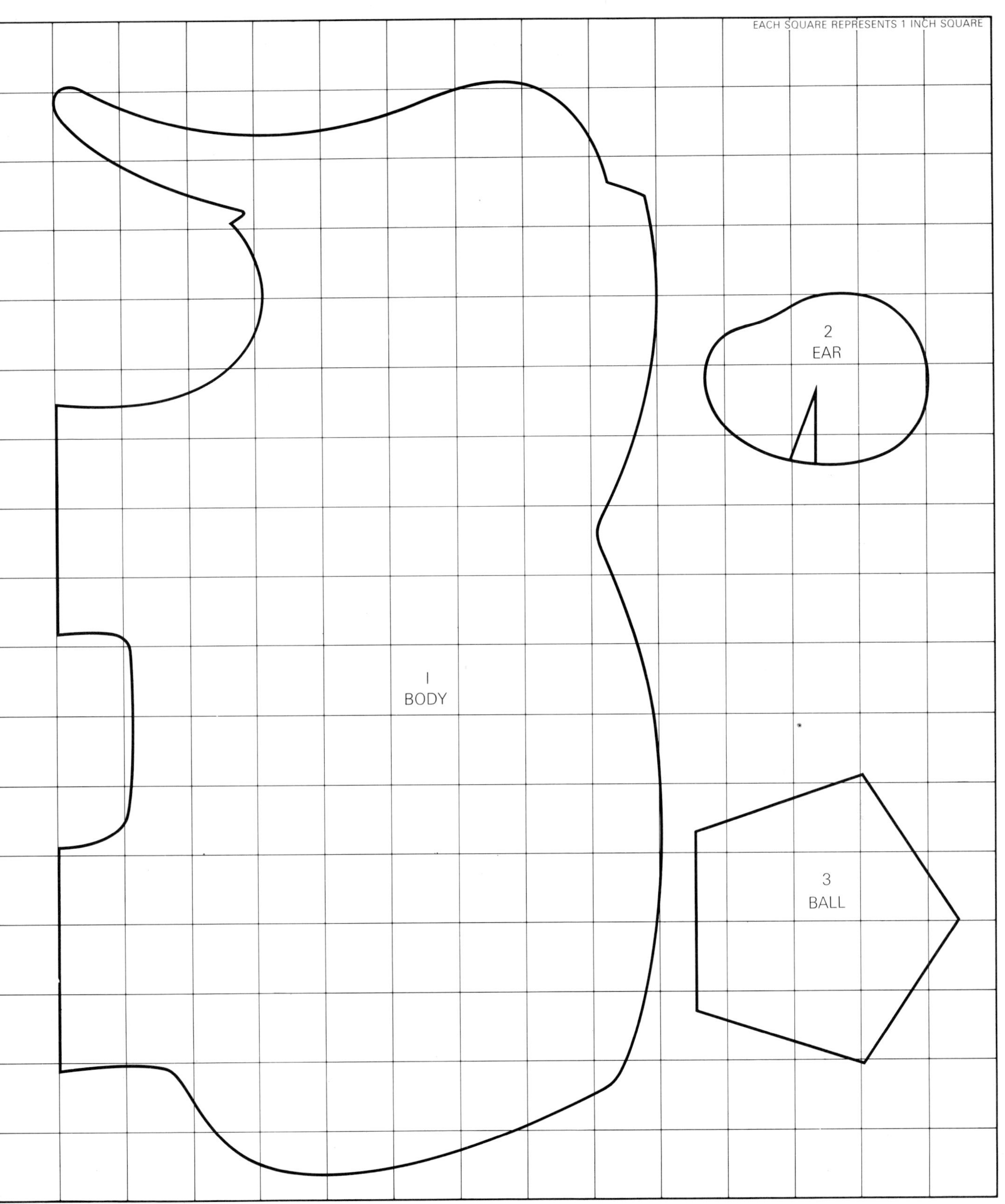
EACH SQUARE REPRESENTS 1 INCH SQUARE
1
BODY
2
EAR
3
BALL

BETA PICTURES

big bun

Warm and woolly, Big Bun is from one of the larger bear families and standing straight is over 3 feet high. A large and dependable companion for children young and old.

Materials required

$1\frac{1}{4}$ yards 54-inch wide Teddy bear fur fabric in main colour
$\frac{1}{4}$ yard 54-inch wide contrasting fur fabric for ears, paws and soles
$\frac{1}{2}$ yard 45-inch wide fabric for trousers
Two 1-inch diameter black buttons for eyes
Synthetic wadding for filling
1 yard $\frac{3}{4}$-inch wide elastic for trousers
Brown wool to embroider nose and mouth
Strong button thread

To make pattern

See Know-How.
The pattern pieces you will need are:
1. Body (cut 4); **2.** Head (cut 2 on fold); **3.** Arm (cut 2); **4.** Ear (cut 4); **5.** Paw (cut 2); **6.** Sole (cut 2); **7.** Trousers (cut 2 on fold).

To cut out

Follow the cutting layouts. The pattern has $\frac{1}{2}$-inch seam allowance included.

Making up

All seams are stitched with right sides together, unless otherwise stated.
Bear: Arrange body pieces in pairs. Stitch inside leg seams A to B and side seam C to D. With right sides facing, slip left body piece into right body piece. Stitch centre body seam in one operation from E to A to E, leaving an 8-inch opening for stuffing.
Stitch shoulder seams and underarm seams.
Set a paw piece into the narrow end of each arm; match the notch to underarm seam and ease the arm to the edge of the paw piece. Stitch.
Stitch the soles to the legs in the same way.
Stitch front and back head pieces together, leaving straight neck edge open.
With the body still inside out, set the head into the neck opening, matching E at centre back and front. Tack and stitch.
Set in arms, matching notch on arm to shoulder seam. Tack and stitch. Sew on buttons for eyes as marked on pattern. Embroider nose and mouth in wool, using stem stitch for the mouth and satin stitch for the nose.
Stuff the arms, head and legs firmly. Stuff the body. Turn in seam allowance and ladder stitch the opening firmly by hand. Stitch ear pieces together in pairs around outer curved edge. Turn to right side. Turn in $\frac{1}{2}$-inch seam allowance on straight edges and stitch firmly to the head.
Trousers: Fold each trouser leg in half lengthways. Stitch inside leg seams, F to G. With right sides facing slip left leg into right leg. Stitch centre seam—H to F to H. To make casing turn in waist edge $\frac{1}{4}$ inch, then again for 1 inch. Stitch close to inner fold leaving a small opening for elastic. Thread elastic through casing and stitch ends together.
Turn under trouser hems for $2\frac{1}{2}$ inches and slipstitch. To make turnups turn hems over to right side for 2 inches and catch stitch at inner leg seam.

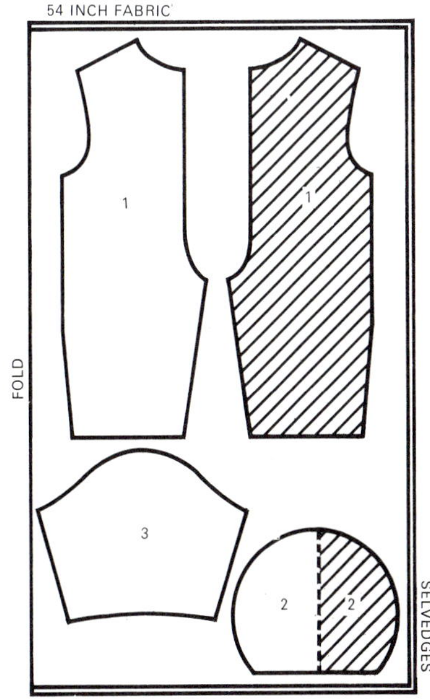

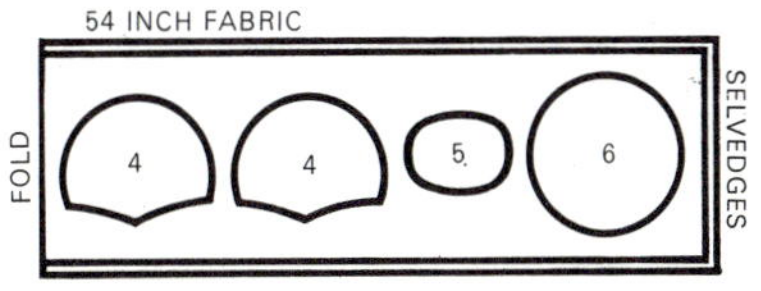

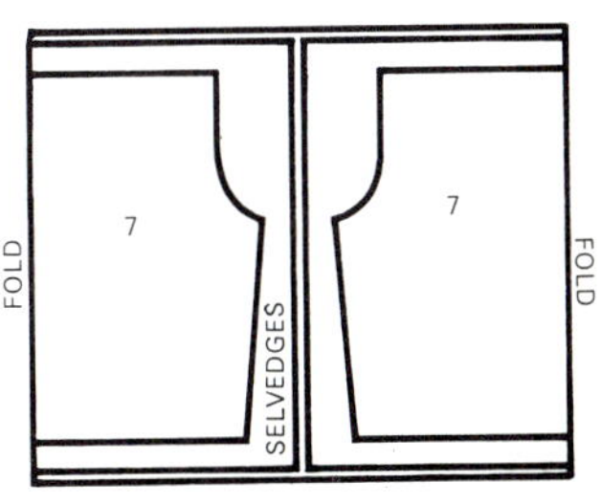

See patterns overleaf

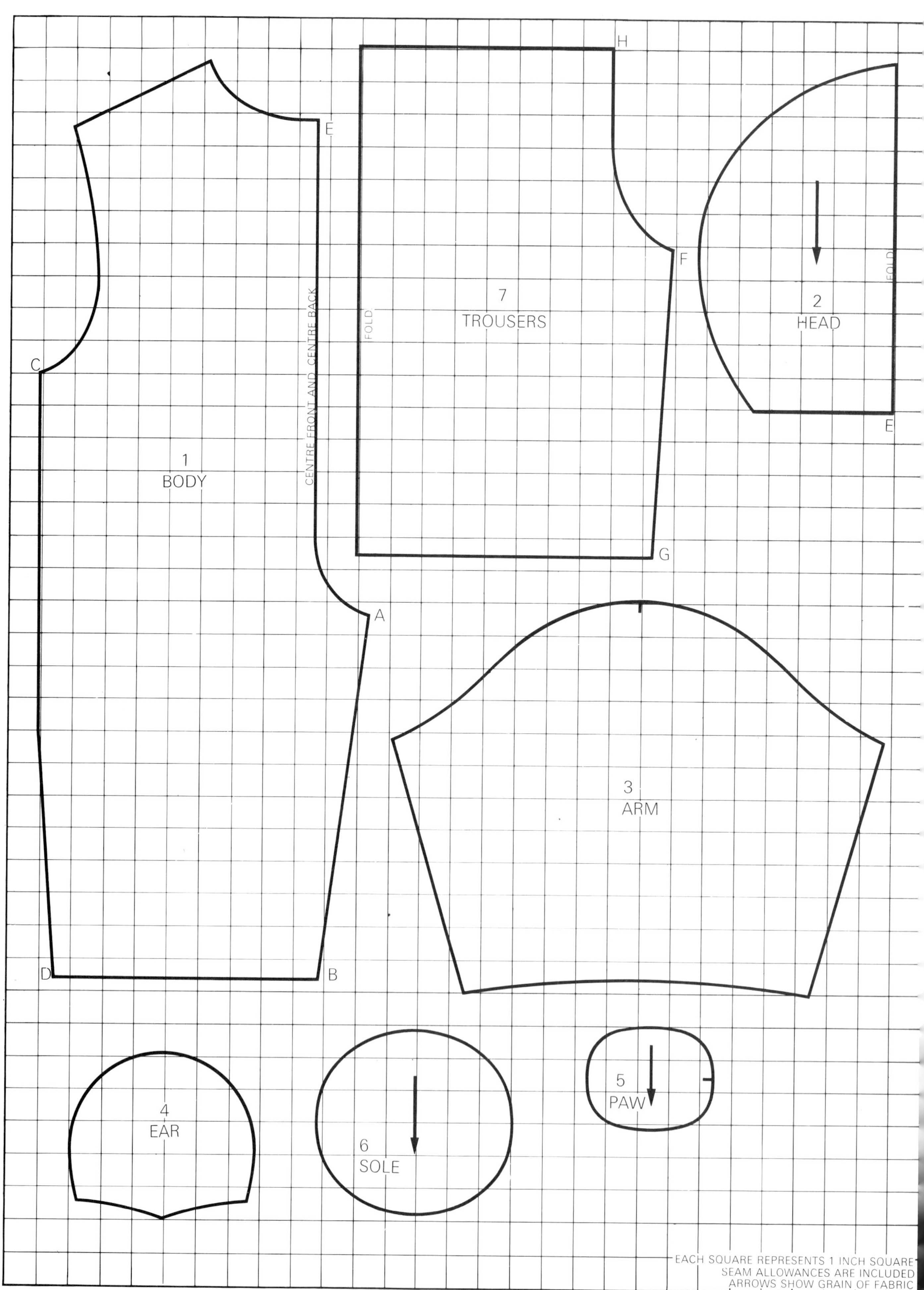
1
BODY
CENTRE FRONT AND CENTRE BACK
A
B
C
D
E
7
TROUSERS
FOLD
H
F
G
2
HEAD
FOLD
E
3
ARM
4
EAR
6
SOLE
5
PAW
EACH SQUARE REPRESENTS 1 INCH SQUARE
SEAM ALLOWANCES ARE INCLUDED
ARROWS SHOW GRAIN OF FABRIC

MALCOLM SCOULAR

freddie the frog

Freddie is 9 inches long and has a patterned back and plain underbody. He is filled with very small beans or lentils. For a really froggy effect white buttons have been used for the eyes with the tops painted black.

Materials required

Two rectangles of firm fabric each 12 inches by 8 inches
Small red lentils or very small beans for filling
Two white dome buttons for eyes
Small tin black enamel paint (optional)
Scrap of black embroidery thread

To make pattern

See Know-How.
You will need only one pattern piece for the frog.

To cut out

The pattern has $\frac{1}{4}$-inch seam allowance included. Cut two frog pieces, one from each rectangle of fabric.

Making up

All seams are stitched with right sides together. Take $\frac{1}{4}$-inch seams throughout.
Place two frog pieces together and stitch all round, leaving AB open.
Turn to right side and fill fairly firmly with beans or lentils.
Turn in seam allowance along AB and ladder stitch to close.
Using black embroidery thread embroider mouth in large back stitches. Paint top of eyes black then sew on eyes to finish.

EACH SQUARE REPRESENTS 1 INCH SQUARE
SEAM ALLOWANCES ARE INCLUDED

FROG
B
A

sarah and sam

The terrible twins, standing about 19 inches high, are a combination of sturdy playmates and soft, cuddly toys. Made in cream calico with thick woollen hair, they possess an unusual charm, while being very easy to make. There are two dresses, equally simple, for the girl doll and traditional denim jeans, check shirt and peaked cap for the boy doll.

The dolls

Materials required

For each doll:
$\frac{5}{8}$ yard 36-inch wide cream calico
1 ounce brown chunky-knit wool
Red embroidery cotton
Kapok for filling
Piece of cardboard 18 inches by 9 inches for girl, 10 inches by 8 inches for boy
Brown or black felt-tip pen to draw eyes
White chalk

To make pattern

See Know-How.
The pattern pieces you will need are:
1. Body (cut 2 for each doll).

To cut out

Follow the cutting layouts. The pattern has $\frac{1}{4}$-inch seam allowance included.

Making up

Place the two body pieces together matching the edges carefully. Tack and stitch all around the edge, leaving a 4-inch opening at the top of the head for turning.
Turn to the right side and stuff the limbs and body firmly with kapok leaving no creases in the material.
Close the open head seam with ladder stitch.

Making the hair

Girl: Wind the brown wool around the 18-inch length of the cardboard tying firmly at one end and winding evenly across the width until the card is covered. Tie off the end.
With white chalk mark a line down the centre of the carded wool, at right-angles to the direction of the winding. This will be the parting in the hair.
Slipping the card off gradually, stitch the strands of wool together down the centre line, feeding the wool closely into the machine. Re-sew several times, each time more closely, until the stitched parting measures 9 inches.
Cut the wool folds at each end.
Position the parting centrally on the head starting 3 inches down from the top head seam, continuing over the head down back of head to neck. Sew parting firmly to head with matching thread.
Draw the hair evenly around the sides of the head, plait each side and tie firmly. Anchor the base of each plait to the sides of the head with invisible stitches.
Boy: Wind the wool round the card as for

CAMERA PRESS

the girl, winding around the 10-inch length of the card.
Stitch the parting as for the girl but make it 4 inches from one side. This shorter side is the front of the boy's hair, the parting being stitched along the centre head seam, not across it. At each end of the parting stitch the strands of wool together so there is no gap in the hair at the sides of the head.
Trim the fringe and trim around the bottom evenly.

The face

For the eyes carefully draw two $\frac{3}{4}$-inch diameter circles on the face and colour with felt tip pen—brown for the girl and black for the boy, as in the photograph.
Embroider the mouth in stem stitch or draw in with red felt tip pen.

Girl's clothes

Materials required

Gingham dress: $\frac{1}{2}$ yard 36-inch wide blue gingham
6 small buttons
6 press fasteners
Striped dress (see cover): $\frac{5}{8}$ yard 36-inch wide striped cotton
$\frac{1}{2}$ yard $\frac{1}{2}$-inch wide bias binding
$\frac{1}{2}$ yard $\frac{1}{8}$-inch diameter silk cord

To make pattern

See Know-How.
The pattern pieces you will need are:
For gingham dress: **2.** Back and Front (cut 1 back with centre back on fold, cut 2 fronts); **3.** Collar (cut 2 on fold); **4.** Cuff (cut 2).
For striped dress: **5.** Back and Front (cut 1 back and 1 front both on fold); **6.** Sleeve (cut 2 on fold).

To cut out

See cutting layout. The pattern has $\frac{1}{4}$-inch seam allowances included.

Making up

All seams are stitched right sides together, taking $\frac{1}{4}$-inch seams, unless otherwise stated.
Gingham dress: Stitch left and right fronts to back piece along the shoulder seams.
Gather lower edge of each sleeve edge to fit the cuff and stitch to the cuff. Turn the raw edge of cuff under $\frac{1}{4}$ inch, fold to inside and slipstitch over 1st row of stitches.
Stitch the underarm and side seams.
Stitch the two collar pieces together along the straight edges and at ends. Turn to the right side and stitch one curved edge of the collar around the neck edge of the dress with ends falling on centre fronts. Turn under $\frac{1}{4}$ inch on the other curved edge and hem to the neck edge on the inside.
Hem lower edge.
Turn in the left and right front facings $\frac{1}{4}$ inch then again for $\frac{1}{2}$ inch and hem, neatening seam allowance at neck edge at same time.
On the right front sew on the buttons and behind each button sew a press fastener.
Striped dress: Stitch the sleeves to the

See patterns overleaf

back and front along the curved edges.
Stitch the underarm and side seams.
Turn under the neck edge twice to make a very narrow hem, and stitch. Hem the sleeve edges similarly.
To make a neck casing for the cord, stitch bias binding on inside $\frac{3}{4}$ inch in from the neck edge. Stitch along both edges of the binding.
For the casing opening make a small hole into the casing on the right side at the centre front. Thread cord through, knot the ends and draw up neck to fit doll. Tie the cord in a bow.
Hem lower edge.

Boy's clothes

Materials required

$\frac{3}{8}$ yard 36-inch wide blue gingham
$\frac{1}{2}$ yard 36-inch wide blue denim
Scrap of bias binding
4 buttons
5 press fasteners

To make pattern

See Know-How.
The pattern pieces you will need are:
2. Back and Front (cut 1 back with centre back on fold, cut 2 fronts); **3.** Collar (cut 2 on fold); **7.** Trousers (cut 2 on fold); **8.** Pocket (cut 2); **9.** Cap section (cut 4); **10.** Peak (cut 2).
Note: follow the dotted hem line on pattern **2** for the shirt.

To cut out

Follow the cutting layouts. The pattern has $\frac{1}{4}$-inch seam allowance included.

Making up

All seams are stitched right sides together, taking $\frac{1}{4}$-inch seams, unless otherwise stated.
Shirt: Make up shirt as for girl's gingham dress but with four buttons and omitting sleeve bands.
Jeans: Fold each trouser piece in half and stitch inside leg seam. The fold can first be decorated with two rows of contrast top stitching if desired.
Turn one trouser right side out and slip inside the other trouser. Stitch the centre seam, from front waist to crotch to back, leaving a 3-inch opening at the back waist. Turn in the edges of the opening $\frac{1}{4}$ inch and edge stitch opening and crotch seam.
Turn in the waist edge $\frac{1}{4}$ inch then again for $\frac{1}{2}$ inch. Topstitch with two rows in contrasting thread as in the photograph. Hem the trousers and pocket tops similarly.
Turn in edges of pockets and topstitch to trousers as the photograph.
Close back opening with press fasteners.
Cap: Stitch the cap sections together along the curved edges.
Stitch the peak pieces together around the long curved edge. Turn to the right side and stitch the raw edge of the peak to the cap edge, right sides together.
Sew bias binding all around the edge of the cap, turn under and hem.
Handkerchief: For the boy's pocket handkerchief hem a 5-inch square of gingham.

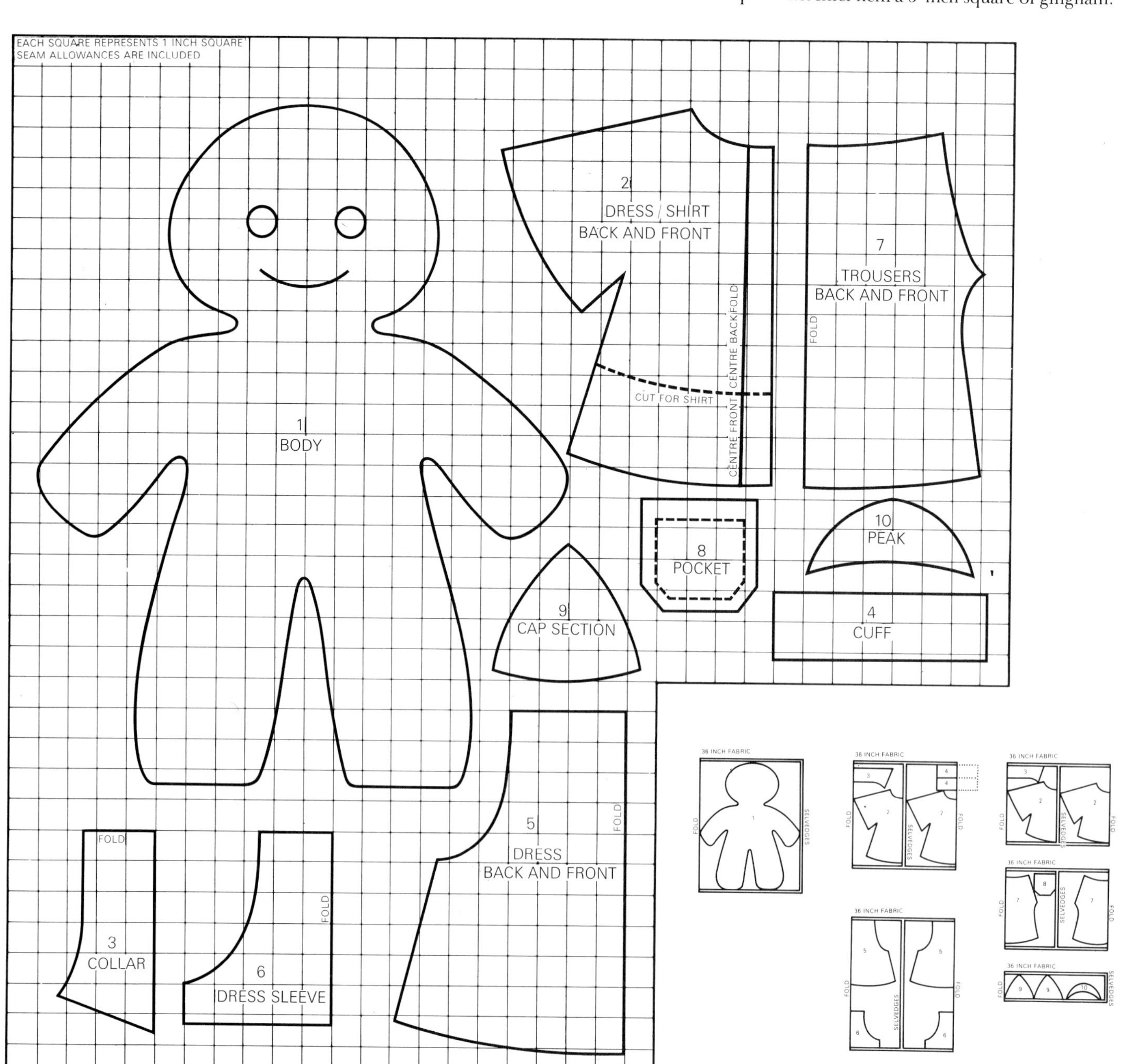

spangles the fish

'his fancy fish measures 16 inches by inches and is very simply made from foam ıeeting. Spangles would make an unusual ecorative cushion for a young child's bed.

Materials required

yard 36 or 45-inch wide main fabric
yard 36-inch wide contrast fabric
r
yard 45-inch wide contrast fabric
$\frac{1}{4}$ yards $\frac{3}{4}$-inch wide fancy braid
'oam sheeting 17 inches by 8 inches, 1 to 2 ıches thick
ıbout 150 small sequins
/Iatching embroidery thread
ıcraps white and black felt for eyes
Copydex or other fabric adhesive

To make pattern

See Know-How.
'ou will need one pattern piece (**1**) for the ish. This pattern does not include seam ıllowance, and should be drawn up without.

To cut out

Position the pattern on the foam sheeting ınd draw round it, using a ball point pen. Cut out with a sharp knife or scissors.
Cut out two fish pieces from main fabric ıdding $\frac{1}{2}$ inch all round for seams.
'or the contrast inset strip between the fish pieces cut a strip of fabric to the thickness of he foam plus 1 inch for seams and long enough to go all round the fish (about 43 inches), joining strips to make up the required length.

CAMERA PRESS

Making up

Sew sequin scales on both sides of fish as in the picture.
Turn in $\frac{3}{8}$-inch seam allowance all round both fish pieces and long edges of inset piece. Tack.
Sew inset to one fish piece all round using a shallow blanket stitch and embroidery thread on the right side.
Place over foam fish, position other side of fish to inset over the foam and sew in place similarly.
Using fabric adhesive stick braid decoration in place on both sides of body.
Cut out black and white felt circles for eyes. Sew together with a sequin in the centre. Stick eye in place to finish.

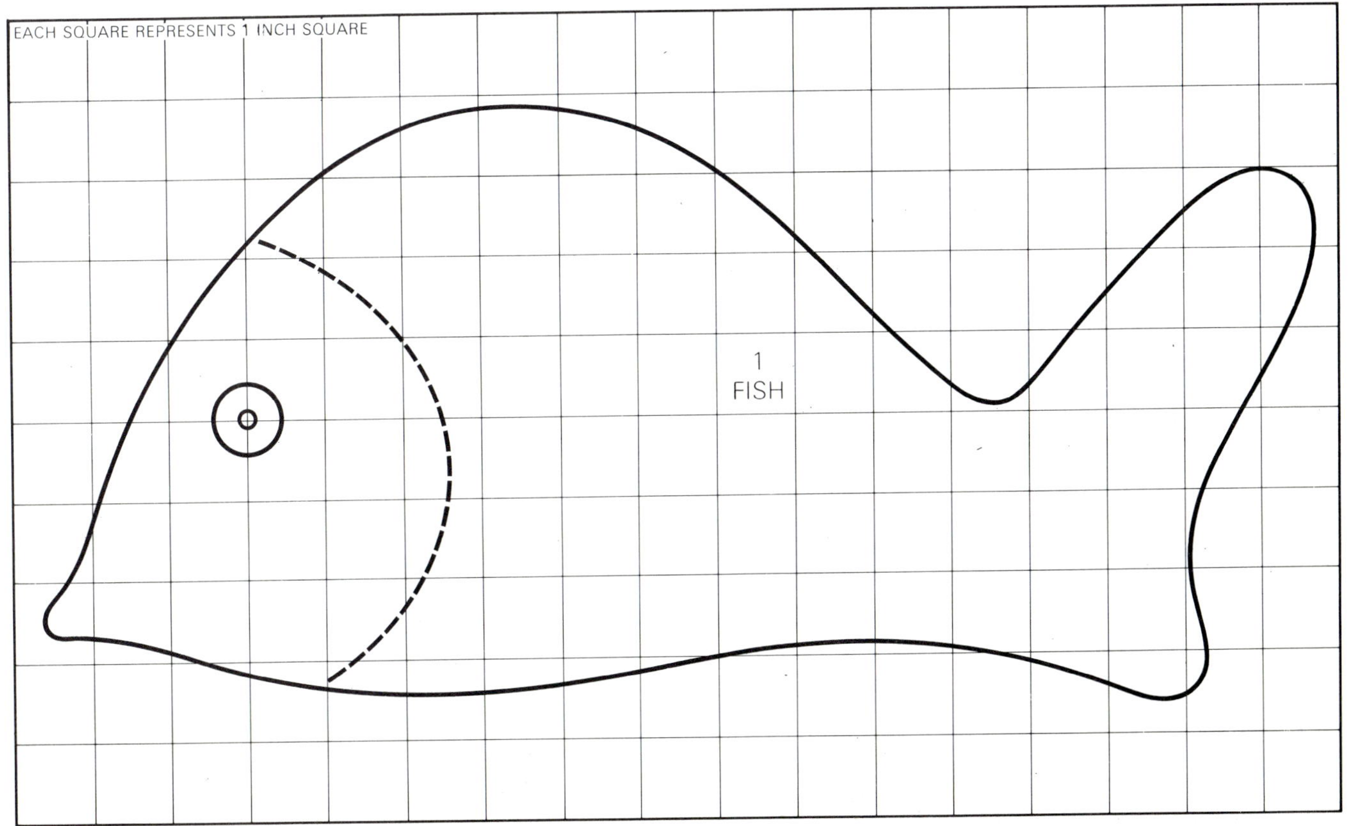

arabella

Arabella is a sedate Victorian lady who would make a fine gift for young and old alike. She has a simple calico body and is about 21 inches tall.

Materials required

Doll

$\frac{3}{8}$ yard 36-inch wide natural calico
Kapok for filling
1 ounce double knitting wool for hair
Piece of cardboard 3 inches by 5 inches
Stranded embroidery cotton in black, pink and red
Scraps of felt in blue, pink and red
Fabric adhesive

Clothes

$\frac{1}{2}$ yard 36-inch wide check cotton for dress
$\frac{1}{2}$ yard contrasting bias binding
1 yard $\frac{3}{4}$-inch wide ribbon for sash
3 small press fasteners
$\frac{3}{4}$ yard narrow broderie anglaise edging
8-inch square felt for boots
$\frac{1}{2}$ yard 36-inch wide white cotton for underwear
$\frac{3}{4}$ yard narrow elastic

To make pattern

See Know-How.
The pattern pieces you will need are: **1.** Torso (cut 2); **2.** Leg (cut 4); **3.** Dress front (cut 1); **4.** Dress back (cut 2); **5.** Dress sleeve (cut 2); **6.** Pantaloons (cut 2).

To cut out

The pattern has $\frac{1}{4}$-inch seam allowance included.
Doll: From the calico cut two torsos and four legs. Using pencil, mark head darts on wrong side of both torso pieces. Very lightly mark features on right side of face.
From felt, cut two pink cheeks, two blue pupils and red lips.
Clothes: From check cotton cut a 10-inch wide strip across width of fabric for skirt, cut off a $1\frac{1}{4}$-inch wide strip from each selvedge edge of this piece for shoulder frills.
Cut two sleeves, one front bodice and two back bodice pieces, taking care to arrange checks attractively on bodice.
From white cotton cut a strip 29 inches by 9 inches for petticoat. Cut two pantaloon sections.
From felt cut out four boots, using leg pattern up to dotted line.

Making up

Doll's face: Working on the right side stick features very lightly to face with tiny amount of fabric adhesive applied with a matchstick.
Using single strand of black thread, embroider a French knot in centre of each eye, surrounded by radiating blanket stitches.
Using two strands of black, outline eyes with chain stitch. Work straight stitches for eyelashes and back stitch eyebrows.
Using single strand of pink, work running stitches round cheeks, one row on felt, one row outside.
Back stitch nose.
With single strand of red, work running stitch and back stitch to emphasize lips.
Body: Working on wrong side, stitch darts on both head pieces.
Stitch round the two torso pieces leaving base open for filling. Carefully clip curves at underarms and turn to right side.
Stitch the four leg sections together in pairs, leaving tops of legs open for filling. Turn to right side.
Beginning with hands and arms, fill doll with small pieces of kapok, pushing it in with wrong end of pencil. Next fill head, neck and shoulders leaving tops of arms fairly soft so that they hang freely. Complete filling of body then oversew base to close.
Fill legs firmly then oversew tops to close.
Stitch legs to base of body with feet pointing forwards.
Hair: Wind knitting wool fifty times round 5-inch depth of cardboard. Remove wool from card, holding it as a skein. Slip wool over head of doll as if it were a turban, arrange to form hair shape then back stitch centre parting. Tuck in ends and stitch to back of head.
Cut four lengths of wool, each 24 inches long. Hold ends firmly in each hand and twist wool. Continue twisting until wool coils up on itself. Arrange as ringlets, tucking in under hair at sides, and stitch to head. Make second set of curls similarly.
Underwear: Hem leg edges of pantaloon pieces. Cut two $6\frac{1}{2}$-inch lengths of broderie anglaise edging and stitch to leg edges. Join the two pantaloon sections, stitching seams AB and CD and leaving gap for elastic at top of one seam.
Stitch inner leg edges.
Make $\frac{1}{2}$-inch casing at waist and insert elastic to fit doll.
Make a 1-inch hem on one long edge of petticoat piece and $\frac{1}{2}$-inch casing on other long edge for inserting elastic. Stitch centre back seam, leaving gap for elastic at top. Press. Insert elastic to fit doll.
Dress: Join front bodice to back bodice pieces at shoulder seams. Press. Bind neck with bias binding.
Bind cuff edges of sleeves. Gather tops of sleeves between notches until they fit armholes. Stitch sleeves to bodice, then join underarm and bodice side seams.
Turn under $\frac{1}{8}$ inch along raw edge of one frill piece, then gather until it fits bodice in half a 'V' shape from front waist to shoulder then down to back waist. Repeat for second frill and stitch frills to right side of bodice.
Make a $1\frac{1}{2}$-inch hem on one long edge of skirt piece. Then stitch centre back seam to within 2 inches of waist line. Press. Gather waist to fit bodice.
Stitch skirt to bodice.
Neaten back bodice opening then stitch on press fasteners.
Cut two strips of broderie anglaise edging to fit sleeves, join into circles and stitch lightly under bound sleeve edge.
Boots: Stitch boot pieces together in pairs, turn to right side. Fit on to feet and stitch to secure.
After dressing doll tie on ribbon sash with bow at centre back.

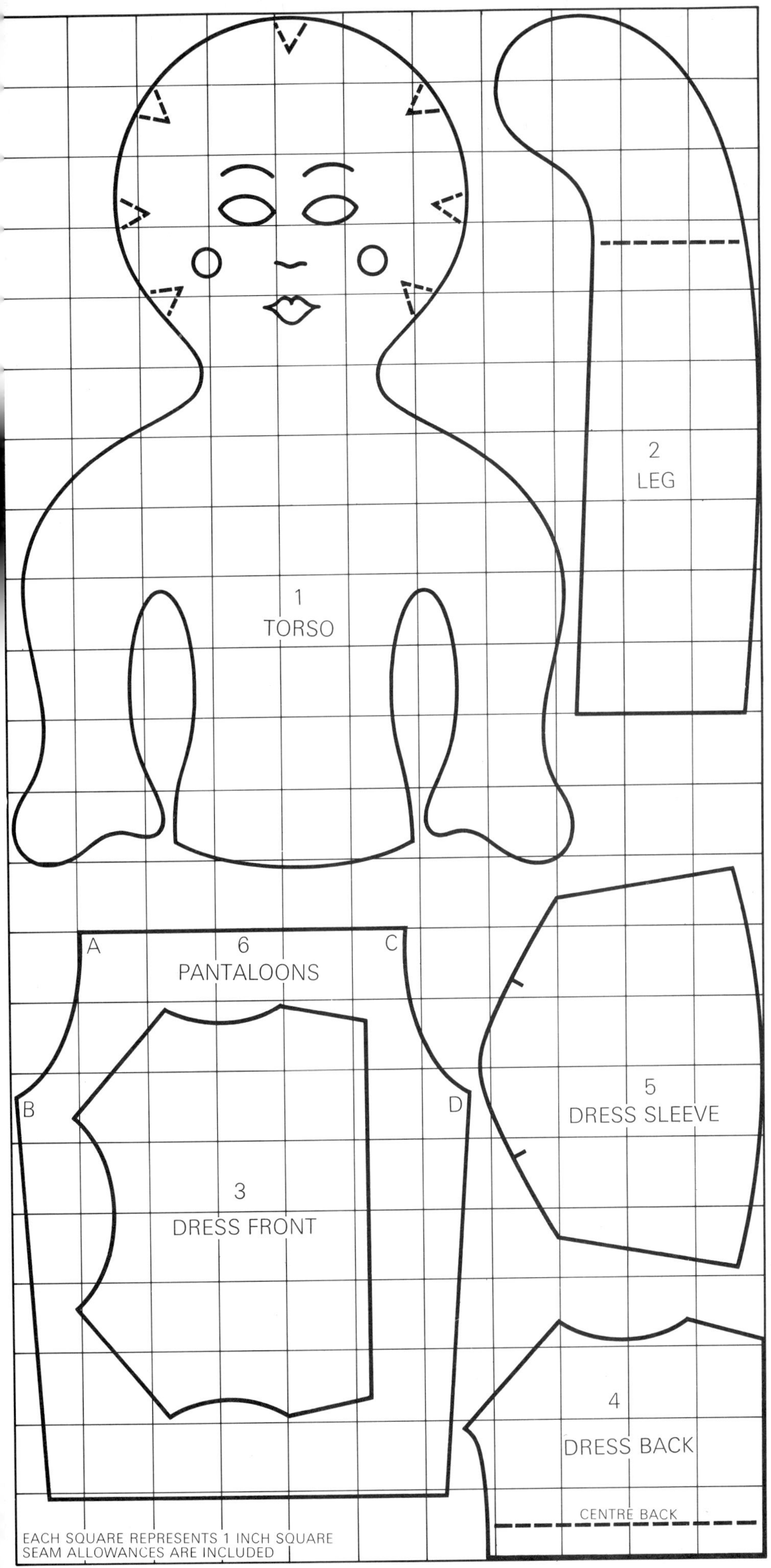
1
TORSO
2
LEG
6
PANTALOONS
A
C
B
D
3
DRESS FRONT
5
DRESS SLEEVE
4
DRESS BACK
CENTRE BACK
EACH SQUARE REPRESENTS 1 INCH SQUARE
SEAM ALLOWANCES ARE INCLUDED

mr and mrs rabbit

Mr and Mrs Rabbit are traditional story book type toys made from grey fur fabric with calico bodies. They are both 16 inches high and are identical except for their clothes.

Materials required

For each rabbit: Piece grey fur fabric 17 inches by 11 inches
Piece white fur fabric 7 inches by 5 inches
$\frac{1}{4}$ yard 36-inch wide unbleached calico
Kapok or foam pieces for filling
Two $\frac{3}{8}$-inch diameter safety eyes
Black embroidery cotton
Mrs Rabbit: $\frac{1}{4}$ yard 36-inch wide cotton print
$\frac{1}{4}$ yard 36-inch wide white cotton
Piece white organza $9\frac{1}{2}$ inches by 7 inches
$\frac{1}{4}$ yard narrow white rick-rack braid
10 inches $\frac{1}{4}$-inch wide elastic
$\frac{1}{4}$ yard white bias binding
$\frac{3}{8}$ yard $\frac{3}{8}$-inch wide white lace
$\frac{1}{2}$ yard $\frac{3}{4}$-inch wide white ribbon
Two press fasteners
Mr Rabbit: $\frac{1}{4}$ yard 36-inch wide gingham
Piece blue felt 16 inches by 8 inches
Piece red felt 10 inches by 7 inches
Piece white felt 7 inches by $1\frac{1}{2}$ inches
$\frac{3}{8}$ yard $\frac{1}{4}$-inch wide red ribbon
$\frac{3}{4}$ yard white bias binding
10 inches $\frac{1}{4}$-inch wide elastic
Four press fasteners

To make pattern

See Know-How.
The pattern pieces you will need are:
For each rabbit: 1. Body (cut 2); **2.** Head (cut 2); **3.** Ear (cut 4); **4.** Head gusset (cut 1); **5.** Arm (cut 2); **6.** Hand (cut 2); **7.** Foot (cut 4).
For Mrs Rabbit: 8. Dress bodice (cut 2 complete patterns for back and 1 on fold for front); **9.** Dress sleeve (cut 2 on fold); **10.** Cuff (cut 2); **11.** Pantaloons (cut 2).
For Mr Rabbit: 12. Shirt (cut 2 complete patterns for front and 1 on fold for back); **13.** Collar (cut 1 on fold); **14.** Shirt sleeve (cut 2 on fold); **15.** Trousers (cut 2); **16.** Waistcoat (cut 1 on fold).

To cut out

Follow the cutting layouts for clothes.
For each rabbit: From grey fur fabric cut two heads (**2**); one head gusset (**4**); two ears (**3**); four feet (**7**); and two hands (**6**). From white fur fabric cut two ears (**3**). From calico cut two bodies (**1**) and two arms (**5**).
Mrs Rabbit: For skirt cut 18 inch by $6\frac{1}{2}$ inch piece of cotton print. Cut remaining dress pieces as shown in layout. Cut pantaloons from white cotton fabric.
For apron, cut piece of organza $9\frac{1}{2}$ inches by $4\frac{1}{2}$ inches and a piece $5\frac{1}{2}$ inches by 2 inches for band.

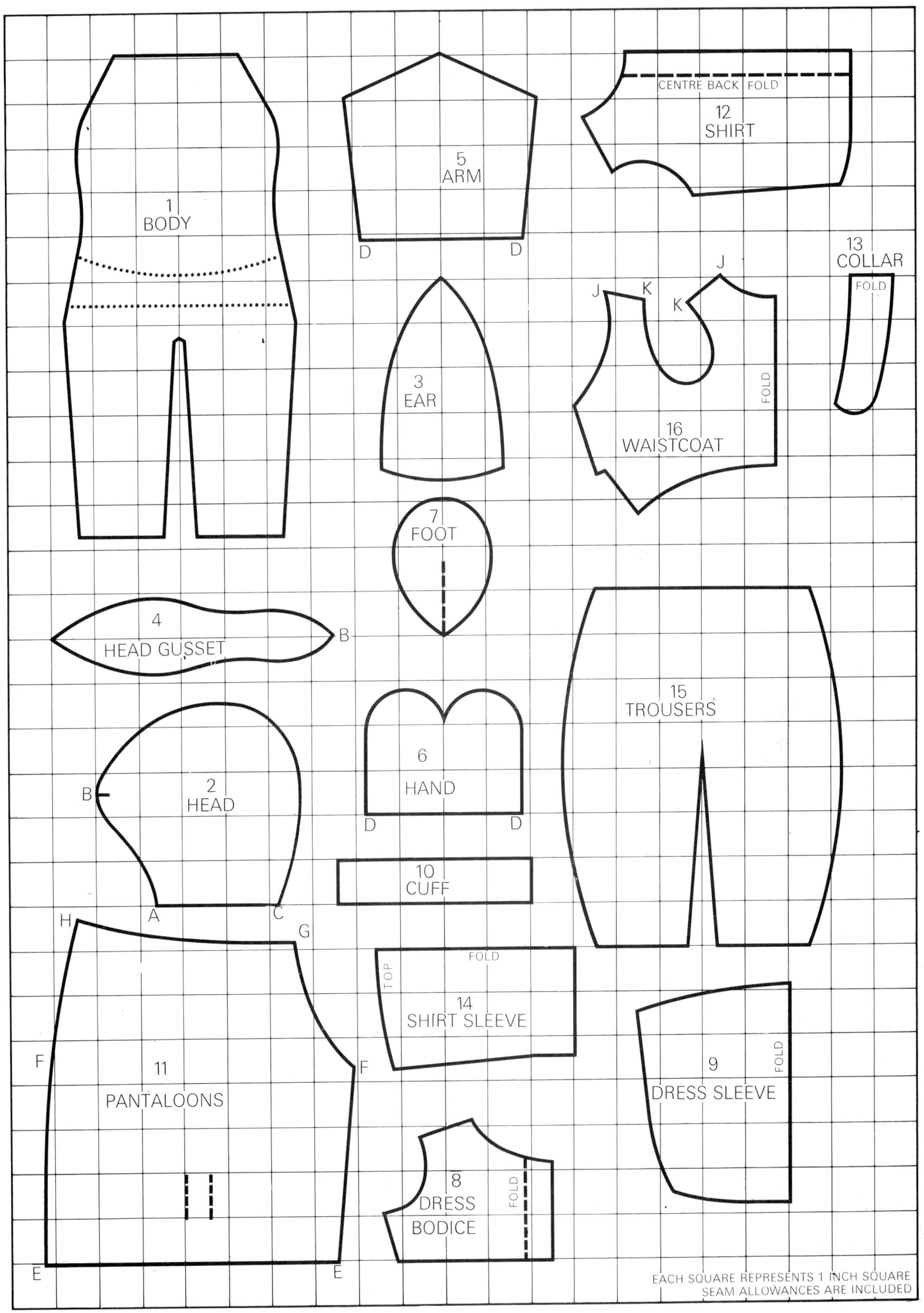
1
BODY
5
ARM
D
D
CENTRE BACK FOLD
12
SHIRT
13
COLLAR
FOLD
J
J
K
K
FOLD
16
WAISTCOAT
3
EAR
7
FOOT
4
HEAD GUSSET
B
15
TROUSERS
6
HAND
D
D
B
2
HEAD
A
C
10
CUFF
H
G
TOP
FOLD
14
SHIRT SLEEVE
F
F
11
PANTALOONS
FOLD
9
DRESS SLEEVE
8
DRESS
BODICE
FOLD
E
E
EACH SQUARE REPRESENTS 1 INCH SQUARE
SEAM ALLOWANCES ARE INCLUDED

Mr Rabbit: Cut shirt in gingham as shown in layout. Cut waistcoat on fold of red felt. Cut two trouser pieces from blue felt. Cut collar on fold of white felt.

Making up

For each rabbit: All pieces are sewn with right sides together, taking $\frac{1}{4}$-inch seams, unless otherwise stated.

Sew calico body pieces together, leaving neck and ankles open. Turn to right side. Sew a line of stitches along both dotted lines, then firmly fill both upper and lower ends of body.

Turn under seam allowance of remaining raw edges. Slipstitch neck edge to close. Gather up ankle edges and oversew.

Sew head pieces together from A to B. Insert head gusset between head pieces, starting at point B. Sew remainder of head down to C, leaving AC open.

Turn to right side and insert glass eyes.

Fill head firmly, then gather opening AC. Oversew head firmly to body.

For each arm sew hand to arm from D to D. Fold hand and arm in half, sew together all round, leaving top edge of arm open. Turn to right side and fill. Turn under seam allowance at raw edges and slipstitch to close. Sew firmly to body.

Place feet together in pairs and slit one piece in each pair along dotted line shown on pattern. Sew together round outside and turn to right side through slit. Fill firmly, then sew to legs round slit in foot.

For each ear place one white ear to one grey ear, right sides together. Sew all round, leaving base open. Turn to right side. Turn under seam allowance at base, pleat slightly and sew to head.

Embroider nose as in the picture.

Mrs Rabbit: Sew shoulder and side seams of bodice and underarm seams of sleeves. Insert sleeves into armholes, gathering slightly to fit.

Join short ends of cuffs. Sew cuffs to sleeves.

Starting 2 inches down from edge of skirt, join short ends of skirt piece. Gather top edge of skirt to fit bodice with opening of skirt corresponding to back opening of bodice. Sew skirt to bodice.

Turn in edges of opening for $\frac{1}{8}$ inch and again for $\frac{1}{4}$ inch and sew. Bind neck with bias binding and sew press fasteners at neck and waist edges of back opening. Stitch hem of skirt.

Hem short sides of apron. Fold band in half, lengthways, and attach it to one long edge of apron, gathering apron to fit. Turn remaining long edge of apron to right side for $\frac{1}{2}$ inch and tack. Stitch rick-rack braid over raw edge. Cut ribbon in half and sew to sides of waist band for ties.

Sew tucks in each pantaloon piece where indicated by dotted lines. With right sides together, fold each piece in half and sew leg seams EF, then sew the two pieces together from G to F and F to H. Make casing at waist and insert elastic. Neaten ankles and trim with lace.

Mr Rabbit: Sew side seams and inner leg seams of trousers. Make casing at waist and insert elastic.

To make waistcoat sew shoulder seams JK and sew two press fasteners at front.

Sew side and shoulder seams of shirt. Sew sleeve seams and insert sleeves in armholes. Turn under raw front edges for $\frac{1}{8}$ inch and again for $\frac{1}{4}$ inch and sew. Sew two press fasteners down front and sew hem.

Bind neck and wrist edges with bias binding. Cut red ribbon in half, sew to each side of collar and tie round neck.

DRESS

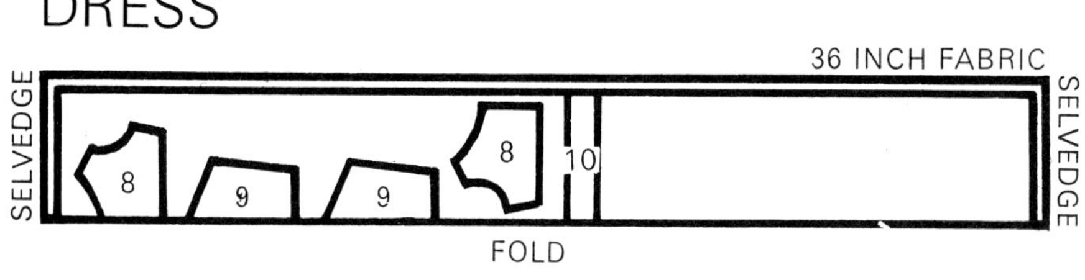

SHIRT

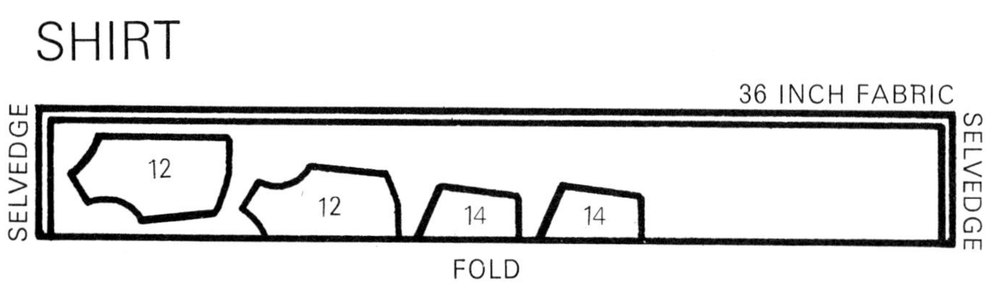

plain jane

Plain Jane is a stocking doll about 21 inches tall. She is very simply made from an old pair of tights. The original doll uses apricot coloured tights inside a lacy beige pair. But if the tights you use are thick enough, only one layer is necessary. The instructions are given for one thickness only. So if you want to make the doll double simply slip the one layer inside the other and work as one.

Materials required

For doll: Old pair opaque tights
Piece dowelling 10 inches long
coloured tights inside a lacy beige pair. But
2 skeins rug wool for hair and an appropriately large sewing needle
Scraps of felt for eyes and mouth
Scraps of soft cotton embroidery thread for cheeks, eyelashes and pupils
Kapok for filling

For clothes: $\frac{1}{4}$ yard 36-inch wide cotton for dress
$\frac{3}{8}$ yard 3-inch wide heavy cotton lace for knickers
Scrap of round white elastic
1 yard daisy lace trimming
$\frac{3}{8}$ yard $\frac{1}{4}$-inch wide narrow ribbon for drawstring round neck of dress
$\frac{1}{4}$ yard narrow ribbon for hair bow

Making the doll

Take $\frac{1}{4}$-inch seams throughout.

Cut feet off both legs of the tights. Cut a piece 21 inches long off one leg and a piece 7 inches long off other leg. Iron pieces flat.

Working on the longer piece stitch the legs as shown in Figure 1. Stitch a 9-inch long 'V' shape from A to B then down to C. Stitch bottom of legs from D to A and E to C.

Cut between the 'V' from lower edge to B. Turn right side out.

Stuff legs firmly and back stitch across top (Figure 2).

Wrap the dowelling firmly with the spare pieces of tights, enclosing some kapok in the wrapping. Wind all round with thread to secure.

Insert padded dowel centrally into remainder of body and stuff body firmly all round dowel.

Run a double thread around the top of stocking and turn in the raw edge. Oversew edges together gathering up slightly to round off the top of the head (Figure 3).

To make the neck, run a double thread round body $4\frac{1}{2}$ inches down from top of head, pull up thread tightly and secure. Wrap double thread round neck, finishing off ends securely, to keep shape of neck.

For the arms cut the remaining 7-inch piece of tights lengthways into two equal pieces. For each arm fold a piece in half lengthways and stitch long edge and one end. Turn to right side.

Stuff each arm firmly, leaving $\frac{3}{4}$ inch unfilled at top. Back stitch across top of filling and stitch unfilled top section to body, so that arm falls about $1\frac{1}{2}$ inches below neck.

To make hair use the needle and rug wool

and embroider loops of wool all over the head, making a back stitch in between each loop (Figure 4).

Following the picture cut out and slipstitch mouth and eyes on face. Embroider eyelashes and pupils and stars (double cross stitch) on cheeks.

To make clothes

Knickers: Narrowly seam narrow edge of knicker lace, turn to right side. Following Figure 5, catch centre of long edges together to make crotch. Run length of elastic round top to fit doll's waist.

Dress: Cut 29 inches off dress fabric. Make $\frac{1}{4}$-inch wide casing along one long edge for neck and $\frac{1}{4}$-inch hem along opposite edge.

Sew daisy trimming down front and along hem. Also decorate with rows of topstitching as shown (figure 6).

Cut armholes as shown, $2\frac{1}{2}$ inches long, $1\frac{1}{2}$ inches down from channel. To find position of armholes, fold centre backs to fall on centre front and centre the armhole slits on the side folds.

Cut lengths of 1-inch wide bias strips from remainder of fabric and bind down centre backs and round armholes.

Run ribbon through casing at top and draw up to fit doll.

Stitch a bow to centre front of hair.

CHRIS LEWIS

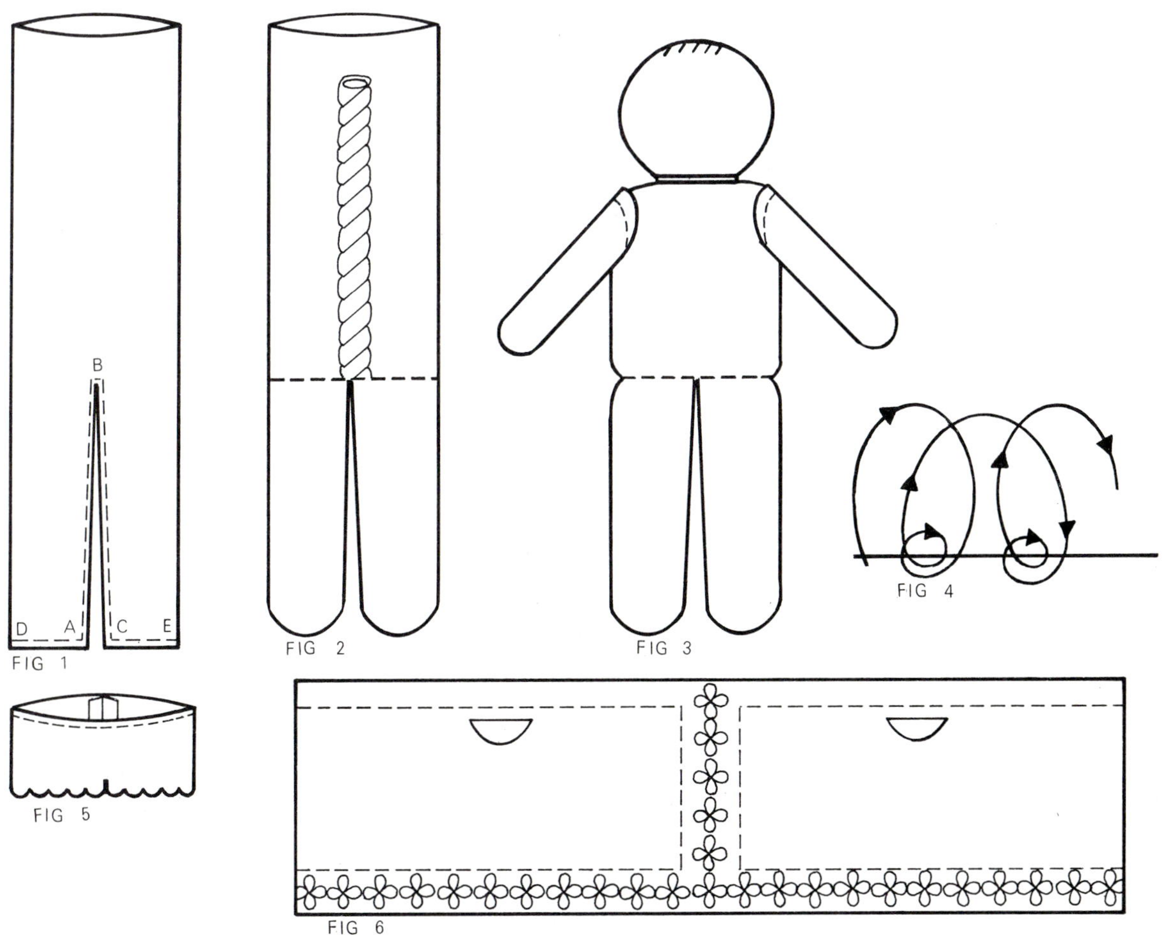

CHRIS LEWIS

bumpy

Bumpy the bear, an animal with great charm, is easily made from fur fabric and felt. He is a cuddly 17 inches high and has movable legs and arms.

Materials required

$\frac{1}{2}$ yard 54-inch wide fur fabric
Two 9-inch squares brown felt for feet and ears
Dark brown double knitting wool for mouth and claws
Four $1\frac{1}{2}$-inch wooden disc joints
Pair of safety eyes
Kapok or synthetic wadding for filling
Strong linen thread
Pliers

To make pattern

See Know-How.
The pattern pieces you will need are:
1. Front body (cut 2); **2.** Back body (cut 1); **3.** Head (cut 2); **4.** Head gusset (cut 1); **5.** Arm (cut 2); **6.** Forearm (cut 2); **7.** Paw (cut 2); **8.** Leg (cut 4); **9.** Foot pad (cut 2); **10.** Ear (cut 4); **11.** Nose (cut 1).

To cut out

See fur fabric cutting layout.
$\frac{1}{2}$-inch seam allowances are included.
Also cut one nose in brown felt. Cut two paws, two foot pads and two ears from brown felt or cut them from the wrong side of the fur fabric, remembering to cut both a left and a right side of each.

Making up

All seams are stitched with right sides facing, taking $\frac{1}{2}$-inch seams, unless otherwise stated. Machine stitch round the edges of all the fur fabric pieces then oversew all the raw edges. This will strengthen the fur fabric and prevent it fraying.

The body: Stitch front body pieces together from C to F.
Stitch back to front body from E to F to E.

Arms and legs: Stitch paw to forearm from Q to P.
Arrange forearm, paw and arm pieces together in pairs and stitch, leaving opening at top as indicated.
Stitch leg pieces together in pairs from M to X and N to Y.
Sew felt foot pads to bottom of legs with a back stitch, matching points X and Y.
Turn arms and legs to right side. Stuff them firmly leaving enough room at the top to insert the joints.

Jointing: Each joint consists of two wooden discs and a cotter pin.

From remaining felt cut eight circles each slightly larger than the wooden discs. Take one wooden disc off each cotter pin and replace it with a felt circle.

On one of the legs push a cotter pin through the fabric from the inside to the outside, where it is marked with a star, so that the felt circle and wooden disc are inside the leg.

Pack filling tightly around the disc and finish stuffing the leg. Turn in seam allowance round opening and slipstitch to close.

Repeat this with the other leg and the two arms.

To join the limbs to the body, again take one of the legs and push the cotter pin through the body of the bear from the outside to the inside where marked. Place a second felt circle on to the cotter pin and then put the original wooden disc back on to the cotter pin so that the second felt circle and wooden disc are inside the body of the bear. Using the pliers, bend the cotter pin open so that the joint is as tight as possible.

The head: Attach one safety eye to each head piece where indicated, using a fixing tool and following the instructions given.

Stitch head gusset between head pieces from A to B on either side. Then stitch head pieces together from B to D and A to C.

Turn to right side and stuff firmly.

Stitch darts in nose piece. Fill nose very lightly then sew in place at A.

Embroider the mouth in wool, using a stem stitch.

Stitch felt and fur fabric ear pieces together in pairs leaving ST open. Turn to right side. Turn in seam allowance at lower edge, turning in the felt slightly more than $\frac{1}{2}$ inch to give the ear a good shape.

Sew ears to head as indicated.

Joining head to body: Stuff body firmly.

Using the linen thread work a row of gathering stitches round the neck opening $\frac{1}{2}$ inch from the edge. Pull up gathering stitches tightly.

Similarly work a row of gathering round neck edge of head and pull up tight.

Turn the seam allowance on the neck edge of the body inside and push the seam allowance of the head inside the body so that the stitching lines correspond.

Firmly oversew the head to the body using the linen thread.

Embroider the claws with double knitting wool as shown.

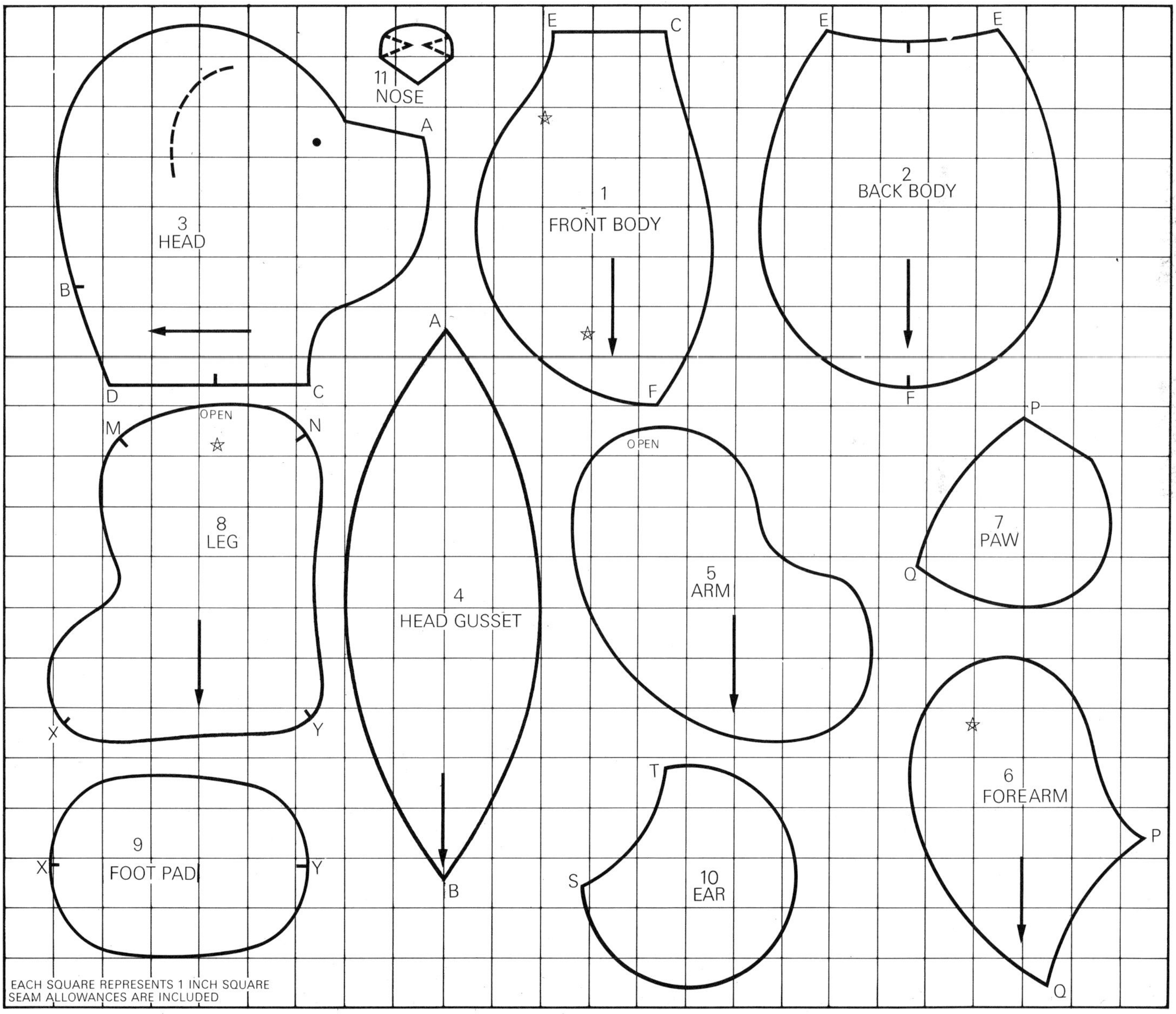

3 HEAD
11 NOSE
1 FRONT BODY
2 BACK BODY
8 LEG
4 HEAD GUSSET
5 ARM
7 PAW
9 FOOT PAD
10 EAR
6 FOREARM

EACH SQUARE REPRESENTS 1 INCH SQUARE
SEAM ALLOWANCES ARE INCLUDED

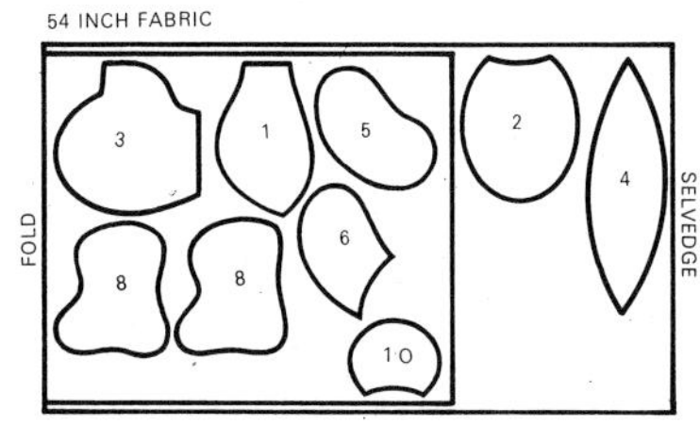

CHRIS LEWIS

flora and butterfly

Flora and Butterfly are two delightfully decorated flat hand puppets. They are surprisingly easy to make and will provide endless amusement to a young child.

Flora

Materials required

9-inch squares felt: two bright blue; two yellow; one bright pink; one orange
Soft embroidery cotton in bright blue and white
Fabric adhesive
Pinking shears

To make pattern

See Know-How.
The pattern pieces you will need are:
1. Body (cut 2); **2.** Stalk and leaves (cut 2); **3.** outer petal (cut 1); **4.** Inner petal (cut 1).

To cut out

Cut two bodies (**1**) from blue felt. Cut one stalk and leaves (**2**) for the back from yellow felt. Trim pattern **2** at AB and cut lower section only from yellow for the front. Cut one solid outer petal in orange. Cut one inner petal from pink. Note the inner edge of inner petal is trimmed with pinking shears so are the edges of the lower leaves both back and front.
Also cut various ovals and crescents following the photograph.

Making up

No turnings are needed.
Position back stalk and leaves to back body. Top stitch stalk in place all round, leaving leaves, from C to D, on both sides unstitched.
Position front stalk and leaves to front body and stitch similarly.
Decorate the lower half of the front with two tiny leaves and pink oval flowers. Slipstitch them in place.
Sew blue veins on back and front in stem stitch as shown.
Place front to back body piece, wrong sides together. Oversew together all round edge of body pieces, leaving lower edge open for hand and leaving leaves free.
To make the flower, place inner petal over outer petal and machine stitch in place close to inner pinked edge with contrasting thread.
Embroider mouth with stem stitch in blue and inner eye with white pupil. Slipstitch eyes and mouth in place.
Using fabric adhesive stick face to front of body.

Butterfly

Materials required

12-inch squares felt: in plum, cerise, and navy blue
7-inch square felt in bright blue
Soft embroidery thread in lime green and scrap in white
Pinking shears

To make pattern

See Know-How.
The pattern pieces you will need are:
1. Body (cut 2); **2.** Wings (cut 2).

To cut out

Cut two bodies (**1**) from navy felt, cut one wing (**2**) from plum and one from cerise felt. Using pinking shears trim $\frac{1}{4}$ inch off cerise wing all round.

Also cut various stripes, ovals and crescents for decoration and features following the photograph and pattern.

Making up

No turnings are needed.

Decorate the right side of back and front body pieces with blue stripes. Stitch them on with a machine zig-zag stitch or straight stitch if you prefer.

Sew eyes, mouth and feelers on front of body with slipstitch. Make small white pupil with embroidery thread.

Decorate front, pinked, wing piece with ovals, again using a slipstitch. Embroider small stars on wing with embroidery thread.

Position front body over front wing, matching points DC. Using a straight stitch on the machine and navy thread, stitch body to wing down both sides.

Stitch back body to back wing similarly.

Place back section to front section, wrong sides together, outer edges level. Starting at point A, stitch all round outer edges to B, leaving AB open for the hand.

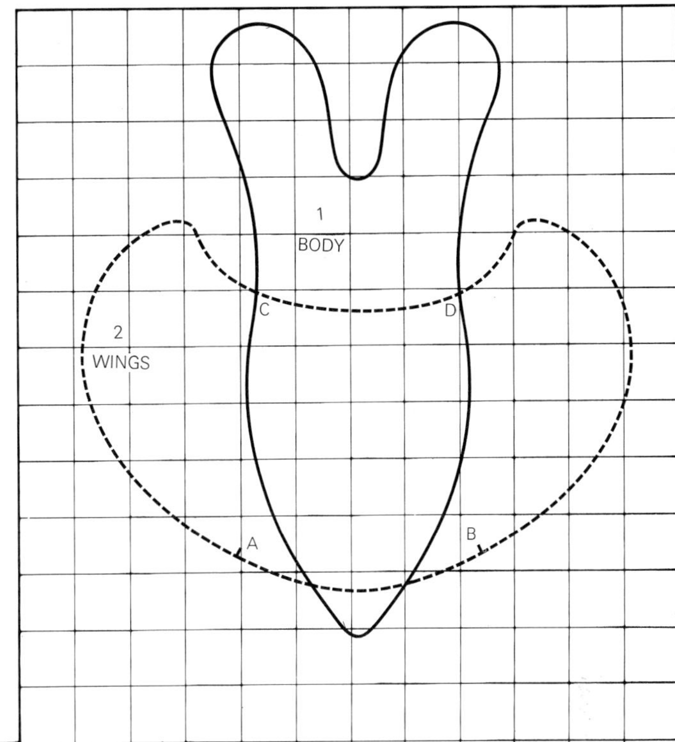

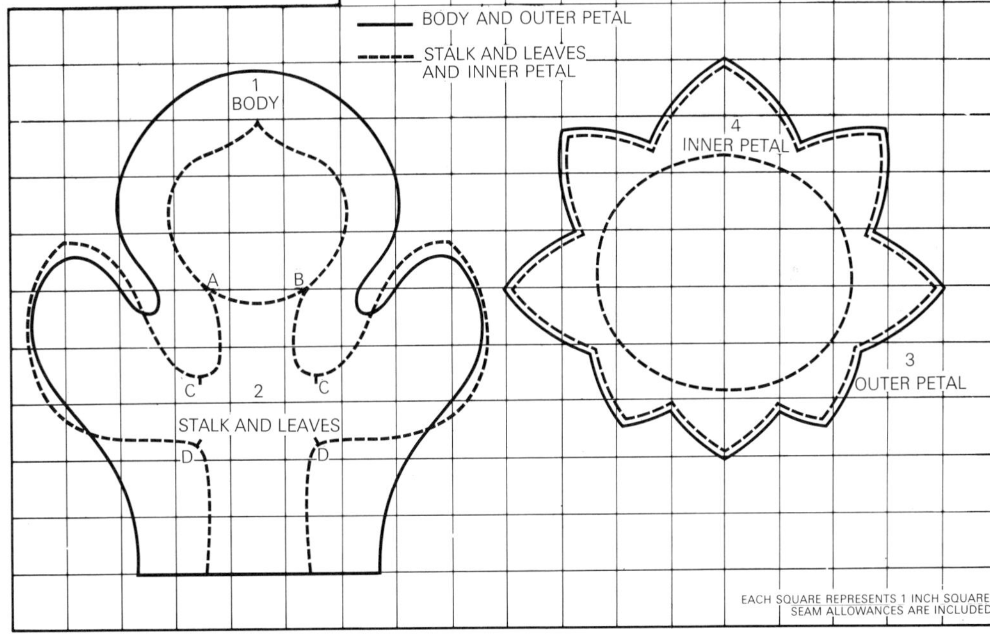

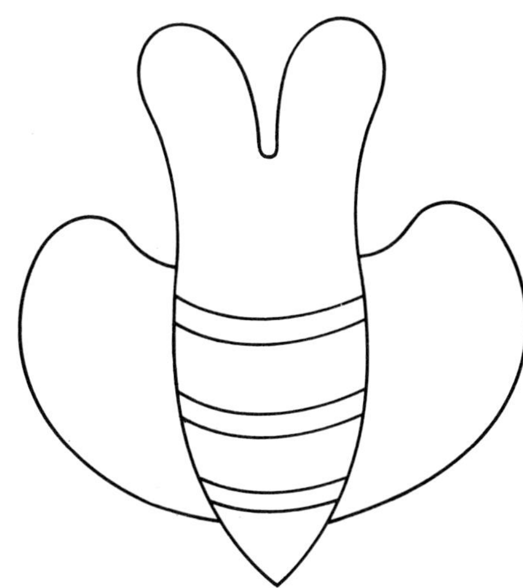

lady laura

Laura the ladybird is 4 inches long. She would make a charming pincushion if filled with sawdust. Another idea is to hang the ladybird from the ceiling on elastic cord.

Materials required

9-inch squares of felt in red and white
6-inch square of felt in black
Two small white beads for eyes
Kapok or sawdust for filling
Scrap of black embroidery thread
Fabric adhesive
Pinking shears

To make pattern

See Know-How.
The pattern pieces you will need are:
1. Body, underbody and wings (cut 4);
2. Nose (cut 2).

To cut out

The pattern has $\frac{1}{4}$-inch seam allowance included.
From white felt cut one underbody (**1**), one wing (**1**) and two nose pieces (**2**). Using pinking shears to shape the wings cut from A to B and trim $\frac{3}{8}$ inch all round outer edge. Also cut two strips with pinking shears $\frac{1}{4}$ inch wide, 4 inches long.
From red felt cut one wing piece (**1**) and trim as above. Still using pinking shears cut two $\frac{1}{4}$-inch strips, one 9 inches long and one 4 inches long.
From black felt cut one body piece (**1**) and seven $\frac{3}{8}$-inch diameter spots. Using pinking shears cut a strip $\frac{1}{4}$ inch wide, $1\frac{1}{2}$ inches long.

Making up

All seams are stitched with right sides together, unless otherwise stated.
Stitch body and underbody together, leaving CD open. Sew nose pieces together leaving straight end open. Turn both to right side and stuff firmly. Position nose to body at CD and oversew in place.

MALCOLM SCOULAR

Using fabric adhesive, stick 4-inch lengths red and white strips over top of body as shown in Figure 1. Stick 9-inch red strip round body to cover seam and short black strip to cover nose seam.
Place wing pieces together, wrong sides facing, and topstitch close to outer edges leaving an opening at the front for filling. Fill very lightly then finish off topstitching. Position wings on body and oversew decoratively to body along ECDF with black embroidery thread.
To finish sew on eyes, embroider feelers in long black threads and stick spots on to wings.

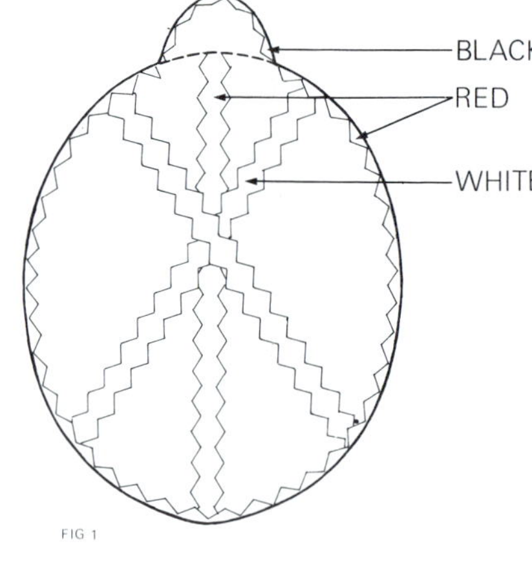

FIG 1

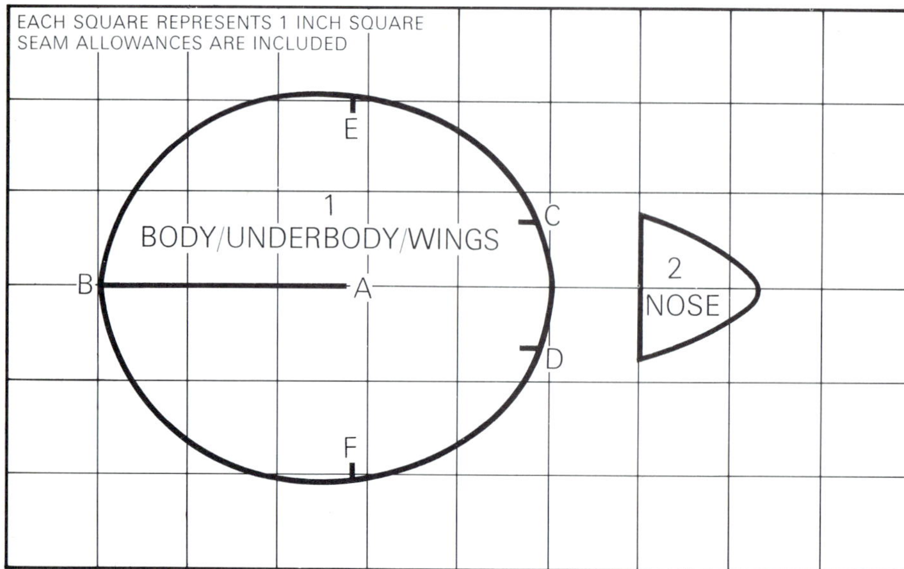

woolly the baby bear

Woolly is a blue and white bear about 10 inches high. He is made in cuddly fur fabric and is washable. There is nothing about Woolly that would hurt a small baby.

Materials required

Fur fabric 24 inches by 9 inches in main colour, with pile running lengthways
Scrap of fur fabric in contrasting colour
Scrap of double knitting wool for features
Synthetic wadding or foam pieces for filling

To make pattern

See Know-How.
The pattern pieces you will need are:
1. Body (cut 2 on fold); **2.** Ear (cut four); **3.** Nose (cut 1); **4.** Paw (cut 4).

To cut out

The pattern has $\frac{1}{4}$-inch seam allowances included where necessary.

From main colour cut out two body pieces (both on fold of double fabric) and two ears. From contrast colour cut two ears, four paws and one nose.

Making up

All seams are stitched with right sides together, taking $\frac{1}{4}$-inch seams.
Stitch round edges of all pieces and then oversew raw edges. This will strengthen the fur fabric and prevent fraying.
Stitch front body to back from point A at base of ear right round body to other ear, leaving top of head open. Carefully snip corners and turn to right side.
Stitch contrast ears to plain ears round curved edges, leaving lower edges open. Turn to right side.
Firmly fill body and ears. Pin ears into position and oversew in place, oversewing opening at top of head to close.
Embroider nose in satin stitch and mouth in stem stitch on contrast nose piece, using the wool. Turn in seam allowance all round nose piece. Tack and slipstitch in place to bear. Sew paws in position similarly.
Embroider eyes in satin stitch to finish.

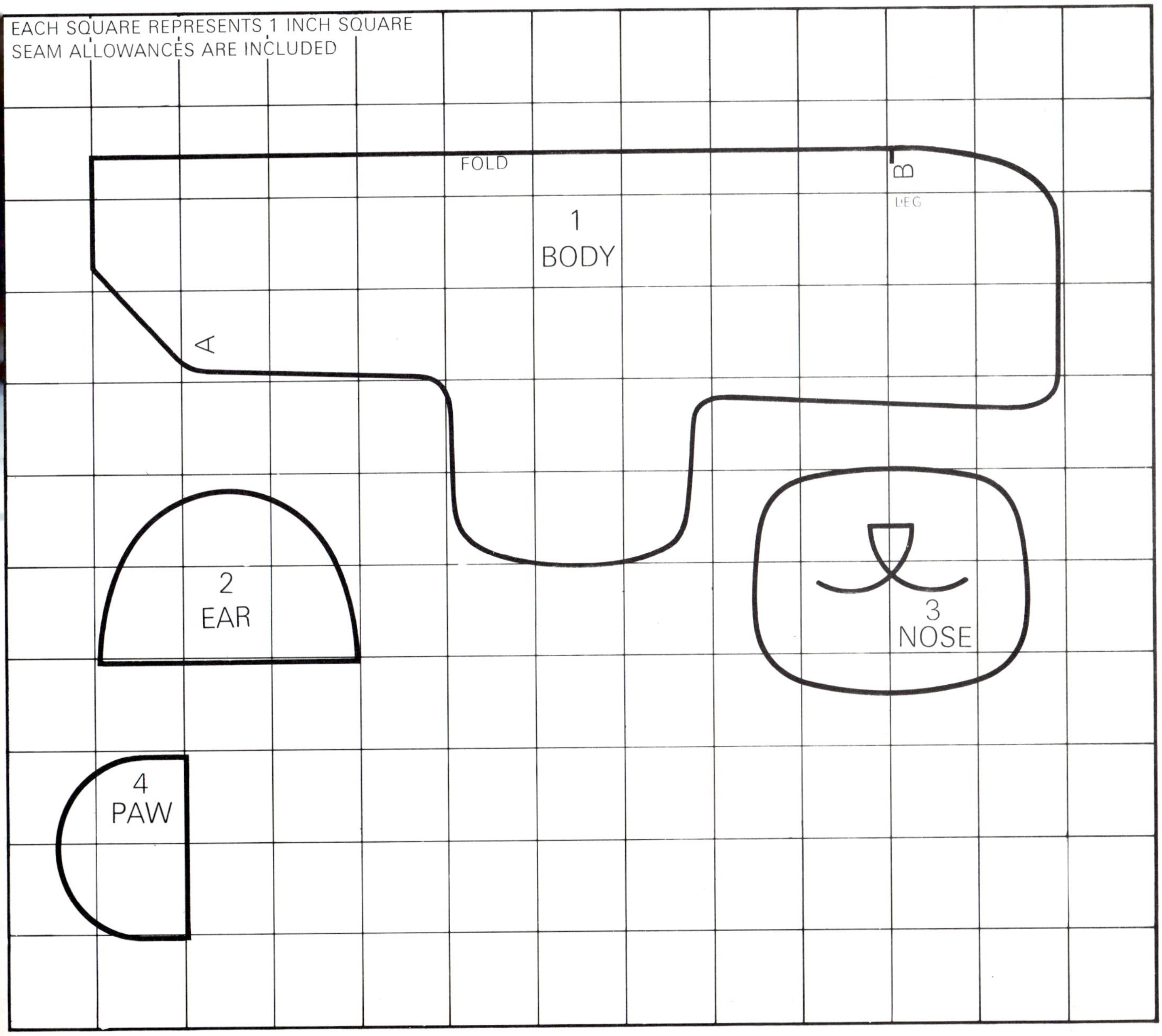

EACH SQUARE REPRESENTS 1 INCH SQUARE
SEAM ALLOWANCES ARE INCLUDED

FOLD
B
LEG
1
BODY
A
2
EAR
3
NOSE
4
PAW

cuddles the puppy

Cuddles is a lovable, floppy-eared puppy with his head on his paws. About 18 inches long, he is made in soft fur fabric, and should prove the most trouble-free children's pet you have ever had.

Materials required

$\frac{5}{8}$ yard 54-inch wide fawn fur fabric
$\frac{3}{8}$ yard 54-inch wide dark brown fur fabric
One 7-inch square of black felt
One 7-inch square of white felt
Scraps of brown felt
Scraps of brown felt or suede for eyelashes
Kapok or synthetic wadding for filling

To make pattern

See Know-How.
The pattern pieces you will need are:
1. Head/body (cut 2); **2.** Body gusset (cut 1); **3.** Head gusset (cut 1); **4.** Ear (cut 4); **5.** Tail (cut 1); **6.** Nose (cut 1); **7.** Eyelashes (cut 2); **8a, b, c, d.** Eye pieces (cut 2 of each).

To cut out

Follow the fur fabric cutting layouts. The pattern has $\frac{1}{4}$-inch seam allowance included. Also cut two foot pads, six toes, one nose and two small eye pieces (**8d**) in black felt. From white felt cut two large eye pieces (**8a**) and two small eye pieces (**8c**), and from brown felt the two medium-sized eye pieces (**8b**). Cut two eyelash pieces (**7**) from brown suede or felt.

Making up

All seams are stitched with right sides together unless otherwise stated. Stitch with a machine or a hand-worked back stitch. Take $\frac{1}{4}$-inch seams throughout.

Stitch the darts on each body piece and on the head gusset.
Set the head gusset between the body pieces, tack and stitch from A through B to C, on either side.
Set the body gusset between the body pieces, matching the paw pieces together, tack and stitch from X round to Y on both sides.
Stitch from A to X under the chin and stitch the centre back seam from C to Y, leaving open from M to N for turning.
Snip around the curved seams, turn to the right side and stuff firmly. Close the opening with ladder stitch.
Fold the tail piece in half lengthways and stitch from O to P. Turn to the right side and fill. Turn in seam allowance on the open end and sew in position at Y.
Stitch the darts on the nose, fill lightly and slipstitch to the head as indicated on the pattern. With black thread, embroider the mouth as indicated on the pattern.
Assemble the eye pieces and sew or stick together. Run a gathering thread $\frac{1}{4}$-inch from the outer edge of the eye. Pull up gently, turning in $\frac{1}{4}$ inch all round. Slipstitch an eye on either side of the head as indicated on the pattern. Stitch or stick an eyelash piece over the upper half of each eye.
Match the ear pieces in pairs and stitch together leaving an opening between S and T. Turn to the right side. Turn in the seam allowance on the open edge and slipstitch firmly to the head on either side, from S to T, as indicated on the pattern.
Slipstitch or stick a black felt pad and three toes to the underside of each front paw, as indicated on the pattern.

leonora the lion cub

Leonora the lion cub is looking rather lost. She is very gentle and soft to touch—an ideal cuddly toy for young children. She measures just over 18 inches long and is made in a brushed acrylic fabric, filled with synthetic filling. The eyes are embroidered circles of felt, making the toy completely safe for babies.

Materials required

$\frac{1}{2}$ yard of 54-inch wide brushed acrylic fabric in gold
$\frac{1}{2}$ yard 54-inch wide brushed acrylic fabric in white
Scrap of light brown felt for nose and eyes
Turquoise embroidery thread
Synthetic wadding for filling

To make pattern

See Know-How.
The pattern pieces you will need are:
1. Body (cut 2); **2.** Gusset (cut 1); **3.** Tail (cut 2); **4.** Ear (cut 2); **5.** Inner ear (cut 2); **6.** Nose (cut 1).

To cut out

Follow the cutting layouts. The pattern has $\frac{1}{4}$-inch seam allowance included. Cut the nose and two $\frac{3}{4}$-inch circles for the eyes in brown felt.

Making up

All seams are stitched with right sides together unless otherwise stated. Take $\frac{1}{4}$-inch seams throughout.
Stitch the darts on each body piece and on the gusset.
Set the gusset between the two body pieces, matching the paws carefully. Tack and stitch

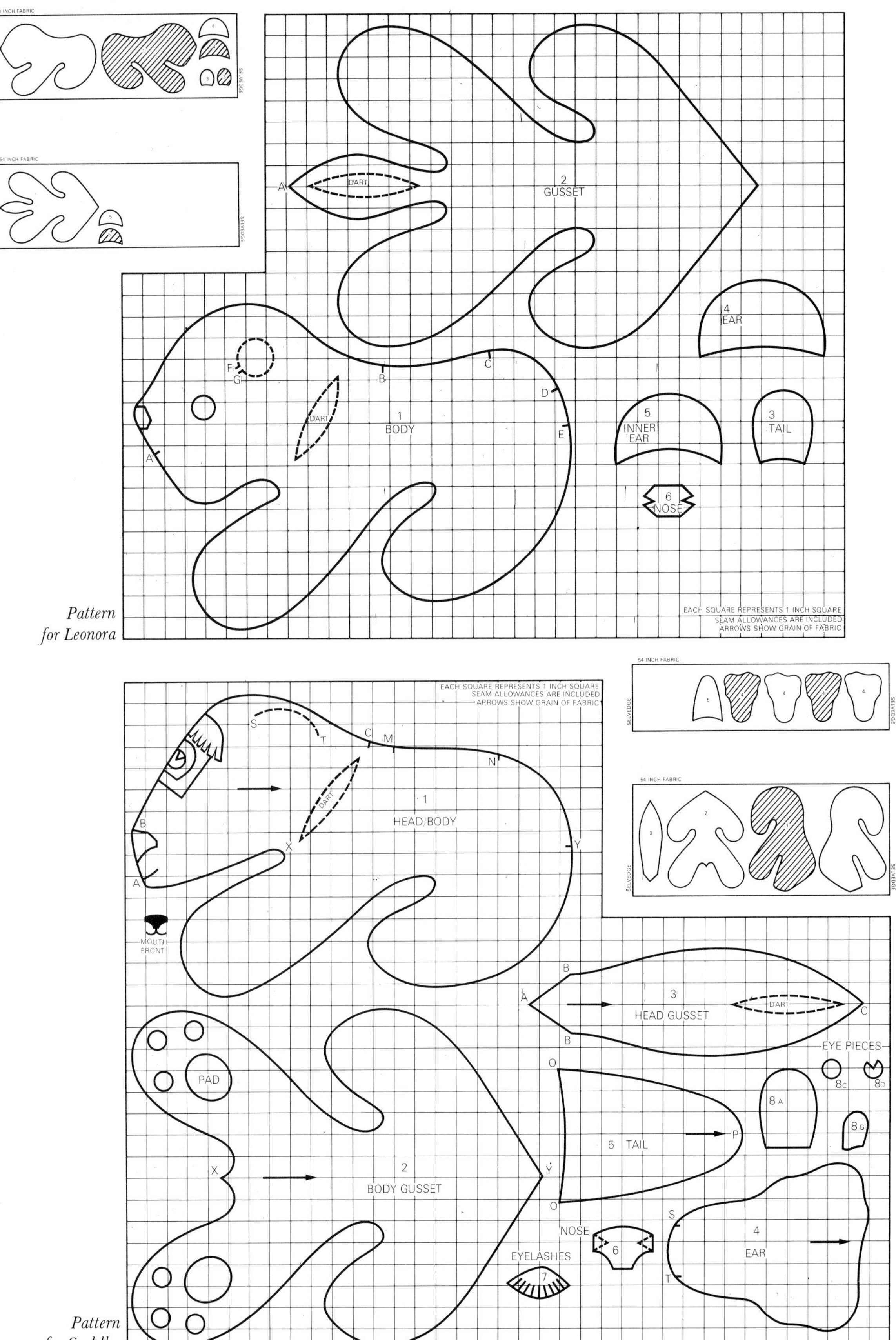

Pattern for Leonora

Pattern for Cuddles

from A around the paws to the end of the gusset on either side.

Stitch the two tail pieces together, leaving the narrow end open. Turn to right side and fill lightly.

Stitch the body pieces together from A to B and from C to the end of the gusset, setting the tail into the seam from D to E. Turn to the right side and stuff firmly.

Close the back seam with ladder stitch.

Tack the ear and inner ear pieces together in pairs around the curved outer edge, easing the ear to fit the inner ear. Stitch and turn to the right side. Turn in seam allowance on the open edges and slipstitch together. Slipstitch an ear to either side of the head, sewing the base in a circle from F to G as indicated on the pattern.

Stitch the darts on the nose. Fill lightly. Slipstitch to the head as indicated.

Buttonhole stitch around felt eye circles in turquoise, leaving a $\frac{1}{4}$-inch diameter circle of felt in the centre. Slipstitch to the head as indicated on the pattern.

CHRIS LEWIS

kitty the puppet

A charming fluffy white kitten which is actually a hand puppet about 10 inches high, made in acrylic fleece or fur fabric. It has a life-like and well shaped head.

Materials required

$\frac{1}{4}$ yard 36-inch wide acrylic fleece or fur fabric
7-inch square of pink felt
Small scraps of pale blue felt
A pair of large blue glass eyes
Synthetic wadding for filling
A piece of thin cardboard 2 inches by 4 inches
$\frac{1}{2}$ yard of $\frac{1}{2}$-inch wide pale blue ribbon
Scraps embroidery thread in pale blue and pink
3 pipe cleaners

To make pattern

See Know-How.
The pattern pieces you will need are:
1. Head gusset (cut 1); **2.** Side head (cut 2); **3.** Side body (cut 2); **4.** Front body (cut 1); **5.** Nose (cut 1); **6.** Ear (cut 4); **7.** Tail (cut 2); **8.** Eye (cut 2); **9.** Paw (cut 2).

To cut out

Follow the fabric cutting layout. The pattern has a $\frac{1}{4}$-inch seam allowance included where necessary.
In the pink felt cut the nose (**5**), two ears (**6**) and two paws (**9**). Cut two eyes in pale blue felt.

Making up

All seams are stitched with right side together, unless otherwise stated.
Head: Stitch the pink nose piece to the end of the head gusset along A to A using very small stitches.
Stitch darts on head gusset and on side head pieces.
Match side head pieces to each side of gusset. Tack and stitch together from A to B on each side.
Stitch the two side head pieces together from B to D and at the front from E to F. On either side of nose stitch to side head piece from A to E.
Turn the head right side out and fill carefully, modelling the shape to look like a real cat.
Roll the piece of cardboard into a tube to fit loosely over your forefinger. Fix with adhesive or sticky tape. Insert the tube into the neck opening, pushing it up into the head. Stitch the edge of the tube to the neck opening to keep in position.
Matching the sides on the ear pieces, stitch pink ear piece to white ear piece for both ears, leaving edge IJ open.
Turn to the right side and turn under seam allowance on raw edges. Position an ear to each side of the head along the side head and gusset darts and firmly ladder stitch in place curving the sides of the ear forward.
On either side of the nose and a $\frac{1}{2}$ inch above it slipstitch the felt eyes in position. Put a glass eye into the head at the centre of each felt eye and secure firmly. Embroider inner corner of eyes with pink embroidery thread.
Using the photograph as a guide embroider the mouth in pink thread using stem stitch. The whiskers are marked by long straight stitches in pale blue.
Tail: Stitch tail pieces together from K to M to L. Turn to the right side. Insert three pipe cleaners folded double in centre of tail and stuff firmly round them.
Body: Stitch side body pieces together along centre back seam, setting the tail in

› the seam about $1\frac{1}{2}$ inches up from the ase.
:itch side body piece to each side of front ody piece sewing from neck edge round :ms to base (that is from G to H).
urn in seam allowance on body neck edge and ladder stitch body neck edge to head, easing to fit if necessary.
Slipstitch pink paw pads in position, one on each paw. Tie ribbon around the neck.
Oversew lower raw edge of puppet to neaten.

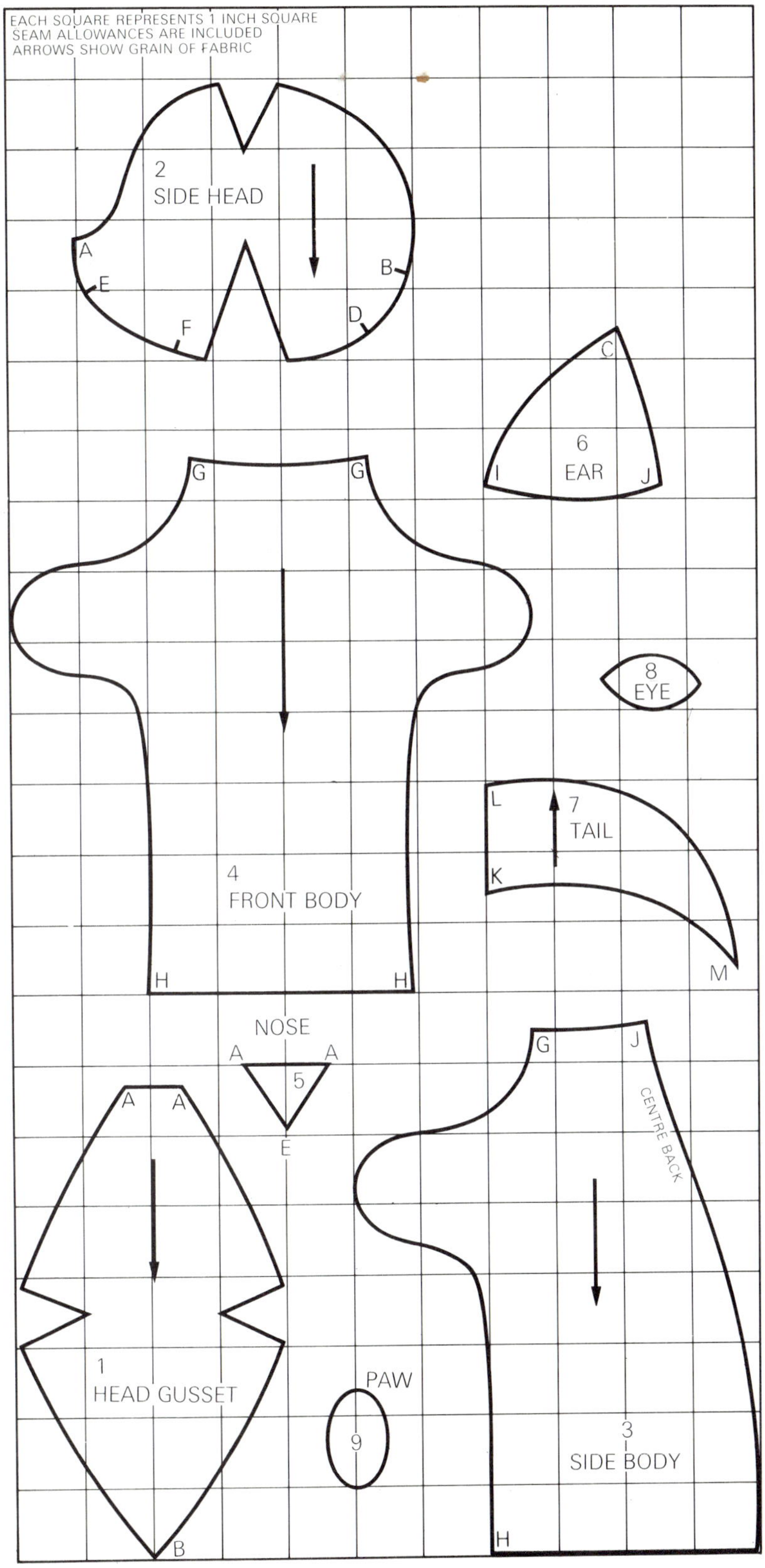

EACH SQUARE REPRESENTS 1 INCH SQUARE
SEAM ALLOWANCES ARE INCLUDED
ARROWS SHOW GRAIN OF FABRIC

2 SIDE HEAD A B E D F
6 EAR C I J
4 FRONT BODY G G H H
8 EYE
7 TAIL L K M
NOSE A A 5 E
1 HEAD GUSSET A A B
PAW 9
3 SIDE BODY G J CENTRE BACK H

36 INCH FABRIC

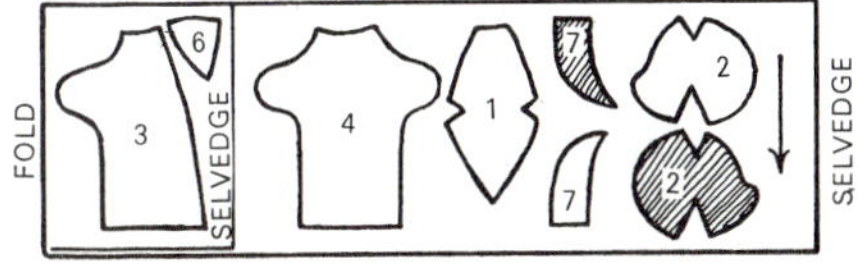

leo the lion puppet

Leo is a magnificent hand puppet and goes well with the cat, but don't forget to think up a lion and cat story before you present these puppets to your children.

Materials required

$\frac{1}{4}$ yard 45-inch wide patterned furnishing fabric
$\frac{1}{4}$ yard 45-inch wide plain furnishing fabric
1 ounce double knitting wool for mane and tail
Scraps of felt in black and yellow
Piece card 3 inches by 6 inches
Scrap of black embroidery thread
Kapok for filling

To make pattern

See Know-How.
The pattern pieces you will need are:
1. Front body (cut 1); **2.** Back body (cut 1); **3.** Outer arm (cut 2); **4.** Inner arm (cut 2); **5.** Head (cut 2); **6.** Head gusset (cut 1); **7.** Ear (cut 4); **8.** Tail (cut 1).

To cut out

Follow the cutting layouts. The pattern has $\frac{1}{4}$-inch seam allowance included.
Also cut eyes and nose in black felt as in picture and four yellow felt pads for each paw.

Making up

All seams are stitched with right sides together, taking $\frac{1}{4}$-inch seams, unless otherwise stated.
Stitch back and front body pieces together along side seams AB and shoulder seams CD.
Place an outer arm to an inner arm, right sides together, letters matching. Stitch from C to X to A. Make up other arm similarly.
Insert arms into armholes with paws curving upwards.
Hem lower edge of body.
Stitch head pieces together from E to G.
Insert head gusset between head pieces and stitch along both sides from G to O to P. Finish head seam from P to H.
Join head to body all round, matching letters.
Stitch patterned ear pieces to plain ear pieces round outer curved edge. Turn to right side. Turn in seam allowance at open end. Gather up base and stitch ears firmly to head.
Stuff head firmly, leaving enough room for 1 or 2 fingers to go right up into the head.
Cut piece plain fabric $2\frac{1}{2}$ inches by 2 inches for inner head tube. Fold lengthways and stitch down long edge to make a tube $2\frac{1}{2}$ inches long. Run a gathering thread round top and pull up to close. Finish off thread securely.
With the body pulled inside out over the head, insert tube into head. Oversew firmly

See patterns overleaf

to the neck edges all round.
Fold tail piece lengthways and stitch long edge. Turn to right side. Turn in seam allowance at both open ends.
Make woollen tassel for tail and insert into one end. Sew other end to back of body.
Sew on black eyes, embroidered with white 'V' as in picture. Sew on nose and paw pads.
Embroider black claws, mouth and eyelashes.
To make mane, wind wool round the 3-inch side of the card till covered, keeping it even and not pulled too tight. Slide off very carefully and machine stitch down centre, making two rows of curls. You will need to make up 6 to 8 such pieces, depending on the thickness of the wool.
Position curls under the lion's chin and all over back of head. Sew in place with matching wool.

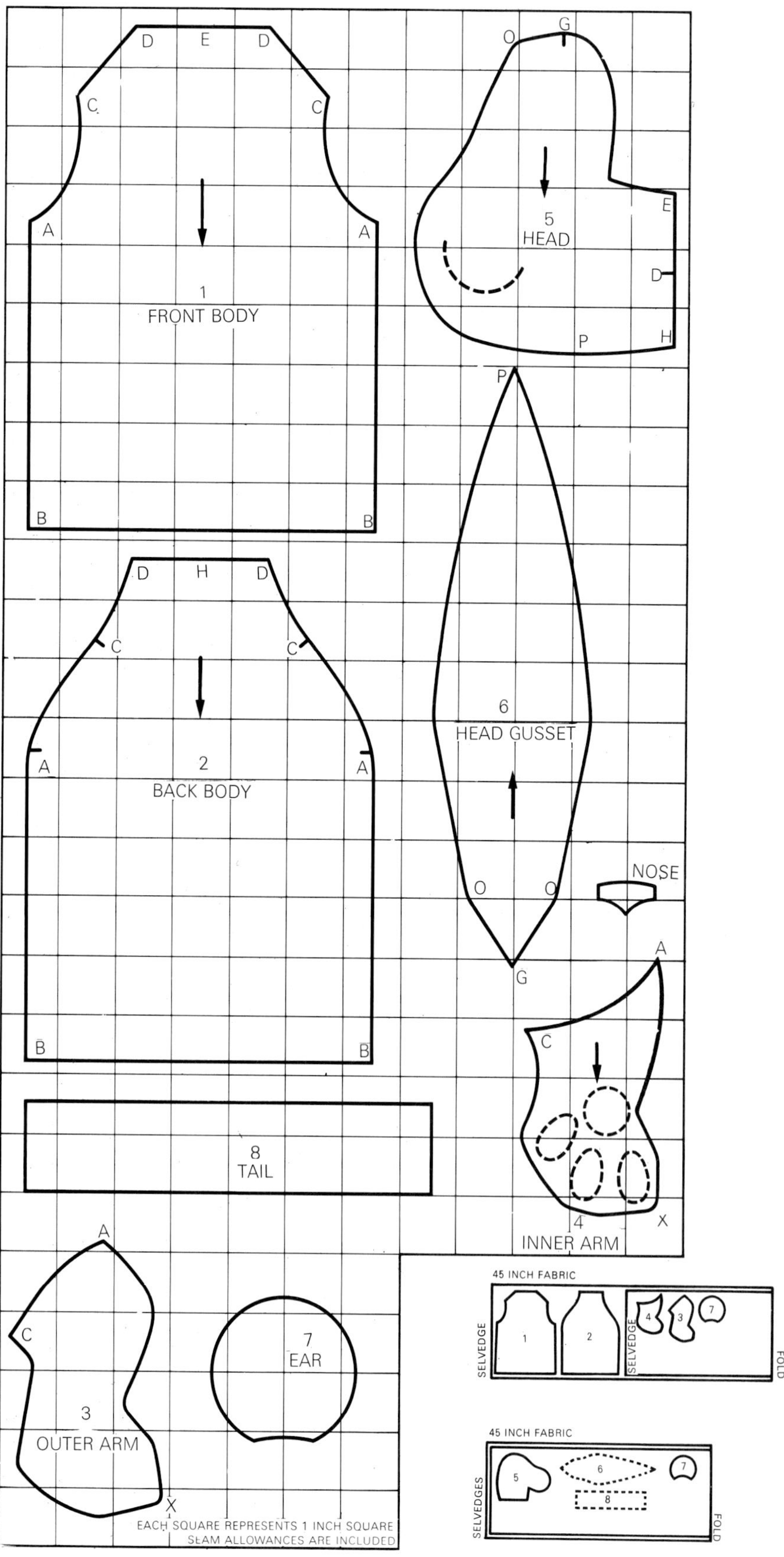

wigwam

An ideal plaything for all children, this wigwam is 46 inches high and roomy enough to play in, and a child could add his own touch by decorating the outside as in the picture. The tent has a window and press fastener opening, but be warned—it isn't water and weather proof.

Materials required

Six broomsticks at least 47 inches long
3 yards 60-inch wide firm fabric such as furnishing calico
Perspex for window 11 inches by 8 inches plus appropriate adhesive
8 large hammer-in press fasteners

To make pattern

Make a triangular pattern from newspaper as in Figure 1.

To cut out

The pattern includes $\frac{5}{8}$-inch seam allowance.
Cut five triangles from fabric, using pattern.
For opening section, cut pattern down centre line and cut each half from fabric, adding 2 inches for turnings down centre edge.
For loops to go round sticks, cut 42 strips fabric (seven for each broomstick) 2 inches wide to the diameter of the sticks plus $1\frac{1}{4}$ inches for seams.

Making up

Stitch seams with right sides together taking $\frac{5}{8}$-inch seams.
On the two opening sections turn in seam allowance down centre line for $1\frac{1}{2}$ inches and stitch. Overlap turned in edges for 1 inch. Starting 31 inches from lower edge stitch together up to the top, leaving lower edge open. For extra strength work another row of stitches $\frac{1}{4}$ inch from first.
Hammer press fasteners down both sides of lower edge to close opening.
On one triangle draw a rectangular window shape, on wrong side, 9 inches across, and 6 inches deep. Cut along this line. Turn in edges $\frac{1}{2}$ inch, and stitch down. Stick perspex over opening to cover seam allowance.
On each loop piece fold long edges to overlap at centre, right side of fabric out, and stitch with two rows of stitches.
Following Figure 2, fold seven loop pieces in half, raw ends level, right side out, and position down one side of a tent piece. Loops should be placed to right side of fabric at equal distances apart, raw edges level with raw edge of triangle. Tack.
Place another triangle on top of this, right sides together. Stitch down looped edge, taking loops into seam. Work another row of stitches in seam allowance $\frac{1}{4}$ inch from first row.
Stitch all pieces together similarly, with loops in between.
Hem lower edge with a 2-inch hem and neaten at the top.
Slot broomsticks through loops.
Make up a long strip of fabric as for loops to tie broomsticks together at top.

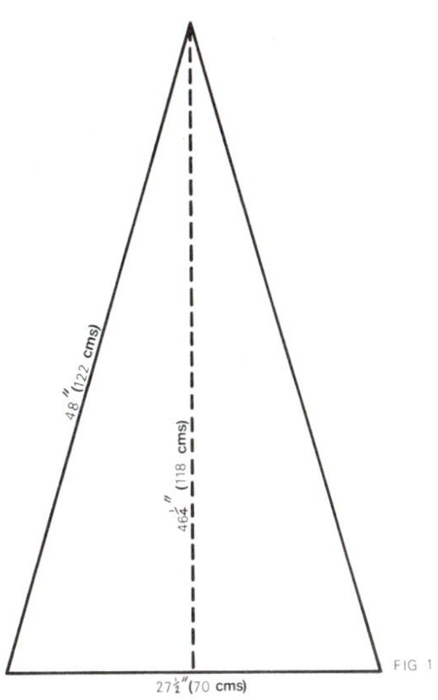

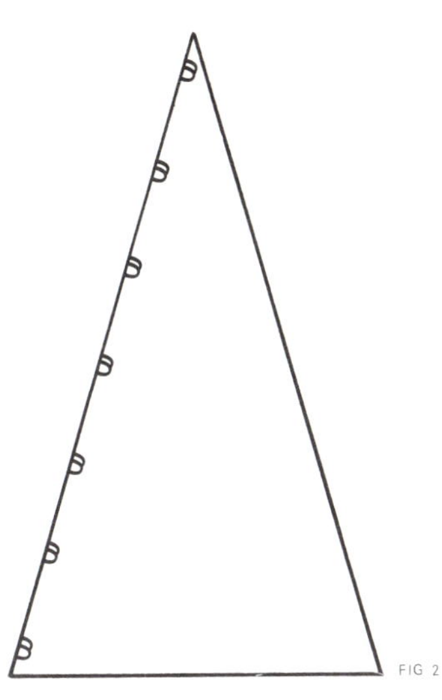

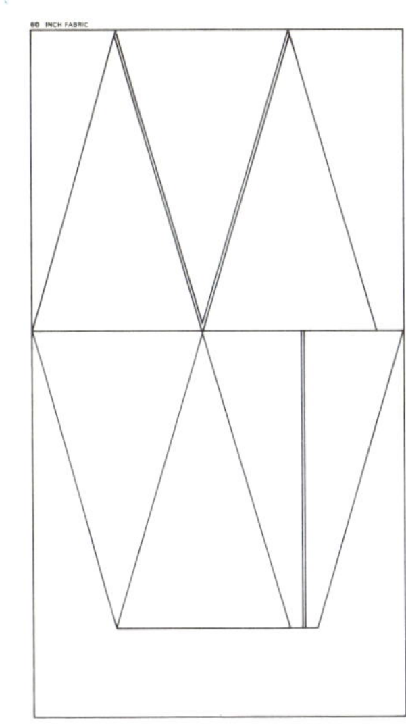

BETA PICTURES

CHRIS LEWIS

flipper the seal

This performing seal makes a splendidly cuddly toy as well as a pyjama case. He is made from soft plush fur fabric and is about 21 inches long.

Materials required

$\frac{3}{4}$ yard 42-inch wide fur fabric
Piece quilted nylon 18 inches by 10 inches
$\frac{1}{4}$-inch thick foam sheeting 18 inches by 10 inches
Scraps of felt in white, black and green for eyes and nose and assorted colours for ball
3 press fasteners
Black button thread
Kapok for filling

To make pattern

See Know-How.
The pattern pieces you will need are:
1. Body gusset (cut 2); **2.** Head/body (cut 2); **3.** Head gusset (cut 1); **4.** Tail (cut 2); **5.** Nose (cut 1); **6a, b, c, d.** Eye pieces (cut 2 of each); **7.** Ball (cut 12).

To cut out

The pattern has $\frac{1}{4}$-inch seam allowance included.
Follow the cutting layout for fur fabric.
The pile should run in the direction of arrows on pattern pieces.
From black felt cut one nose (**5**) and two eye pieces **6c**. From white felt cut two eye pieces **6a** and two **6d**. From green felt cut two eye pieces **6b**. Cut out 12 ball pieces from assorted scraps felt.

Making up

All seams are first tacked then sewn with a back stitch, right sides together, unless otherwise stated.
Place body gusset pieces together and sew from D to C and B to A.
Match body gusset to head/body pieces and sew from A to D on each side.
Sew head together from D to E.
Position the head gusset between head pieces and sew from E to F on each side.
Sew back from F to G and tail from A to H.
Place tail pieces together and sew from H to G. Position between body tail section, matching letters. Sew, then turn seal right side out. Fill flippers fairly lightly then sew across from L to M.
Stuff tail section firmly as far as indicated by dotted line on the pattern. Deal with head in same way.
To make inner bag for pyjamas lay foam sheeting down with quilting right side up over it. Fold in half to make 9 inches by 10 inches, with quilting inside.
Starting from fold, machine stitch down each side. Leave edge opposite fold open.
Insert bag into body of seal, securing it with a stitch in the places marked X.
Turn in small hem on both fur fabric and bag and slipstitch the two together round the opening. Sew on press fasteners to close.
Assemble the eye pieces and sew together. Run a gathering thread close to outside of largest piece. Pull up slightly and secure thread. Slipstitch eyes in place.
Sew on black felt nose and embroider mouth.
On the body pattern there are four dots marked on the seal's tail. Using button thread stitch on one side of seal through dots joining 1 to 2 and 3 to 4, pull up stitches and end off firmly. Repeat on other side. This makes the tail open out.
Ball: The ball pieces can be machine zig-zagged or oversewn together.
Make up one half of ball by sewing one pentagon of felt to each side of a central pentagon. Then sew outer ones to each other at adjacent sides, thus forming a cup. Do the same with remaining six.
Sew the two cups together leaving one side open. Fill lightly and close opening.
Sew ball to seal just above his nose.

42 INCH FABRIC
SELVEDGE
SELVEDGE

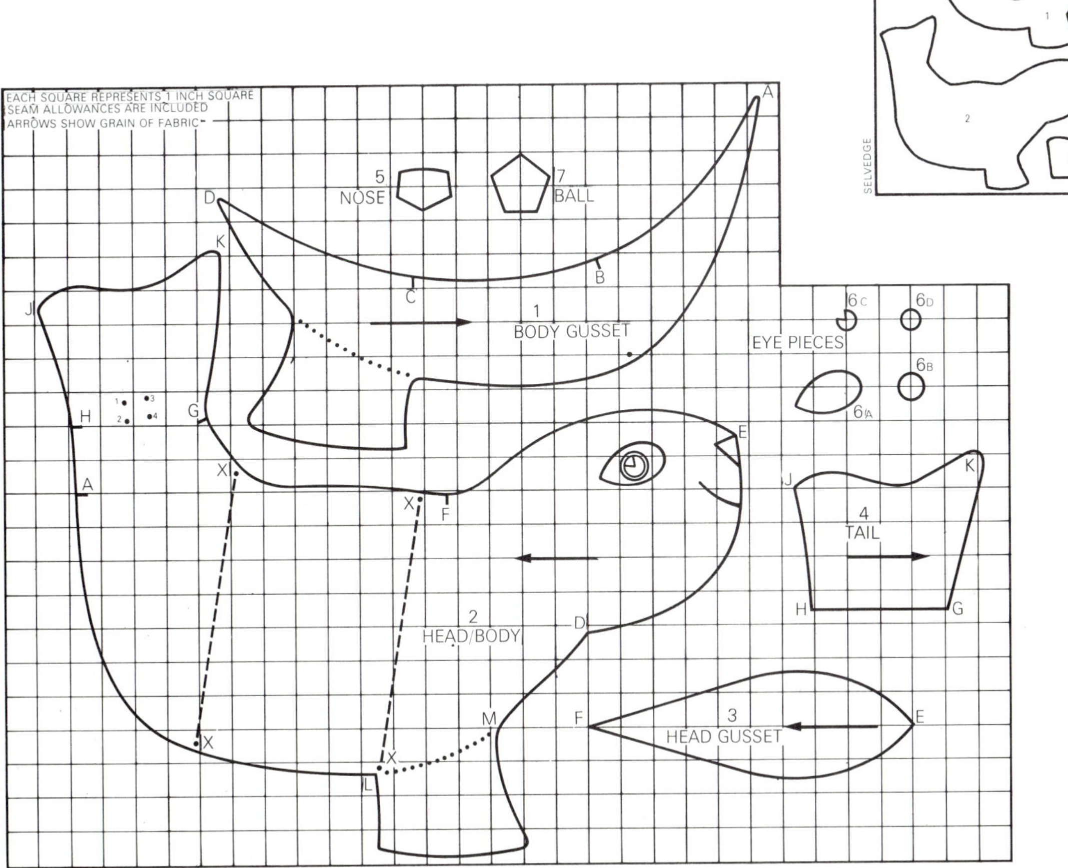

pickles the pony

CAMERA PRESS

See instructions overleaf

pickles the pony

Pickles is a gay little gingham pony about 6 inches high.

Materials required

$\frac{1}{4}$ yard 36-inch wide gingham
Scraps of felt for ears and eyes
Double knitting wool for mane and tail
Synthetic wadding or foam pieces for filling

To make pattern

See Know-How.
The pattern pieces you will need are:
1. Body (cut 2); **2.** Gusset (cut 2); **3.** Forehead (cut 1); **4.** Ear (cut 4).
For the body pattern follow the complete outline of pony. For the gusset follow the section below the dotted line AB.

To cut out

The pattern has $\frac{1}{4}$-inch seam allowance included.
From gingham cut out two body pieces, two gussets and one forehead.
From felt cut out four ears.

Making up

All seams are stitched with right sides together, taking $\frac{1}{4}$-inch seams, unless otherwise stated.
Join the two gusset sections together from A to B.
Starting at A and working round legs to B, join gusset to both halves of body.
Stitch forehead to both body pieces from C to D, leaving $\frac{1}{2}$-inch openings for inserting ears at top of gusset.
Stitch chin seam from A to C, then join back from B to E, leaving DE open for filling.
Carefully snip curved seams under chin and stomach and turn to right side.
Oversew ears together in pairs.
Firmly fill body, pushing filling in with wrong end of pencil. Oversew neck opening to close.
Position ears as in the picture and stitch in place.
Cut out two eyes from felt and stitch in place.
Using a darning needle sew several long strands of wool to tail point. Plait them. Knot the end and trim.
Cut a rectangle of cardboard $1\frac{1}{4}$ inches by 4 inches and wind wool round thickly for mane. Back stitch along one edge to secure, then cut wool along other edge. Secure any loose strands and stitch mane in position.

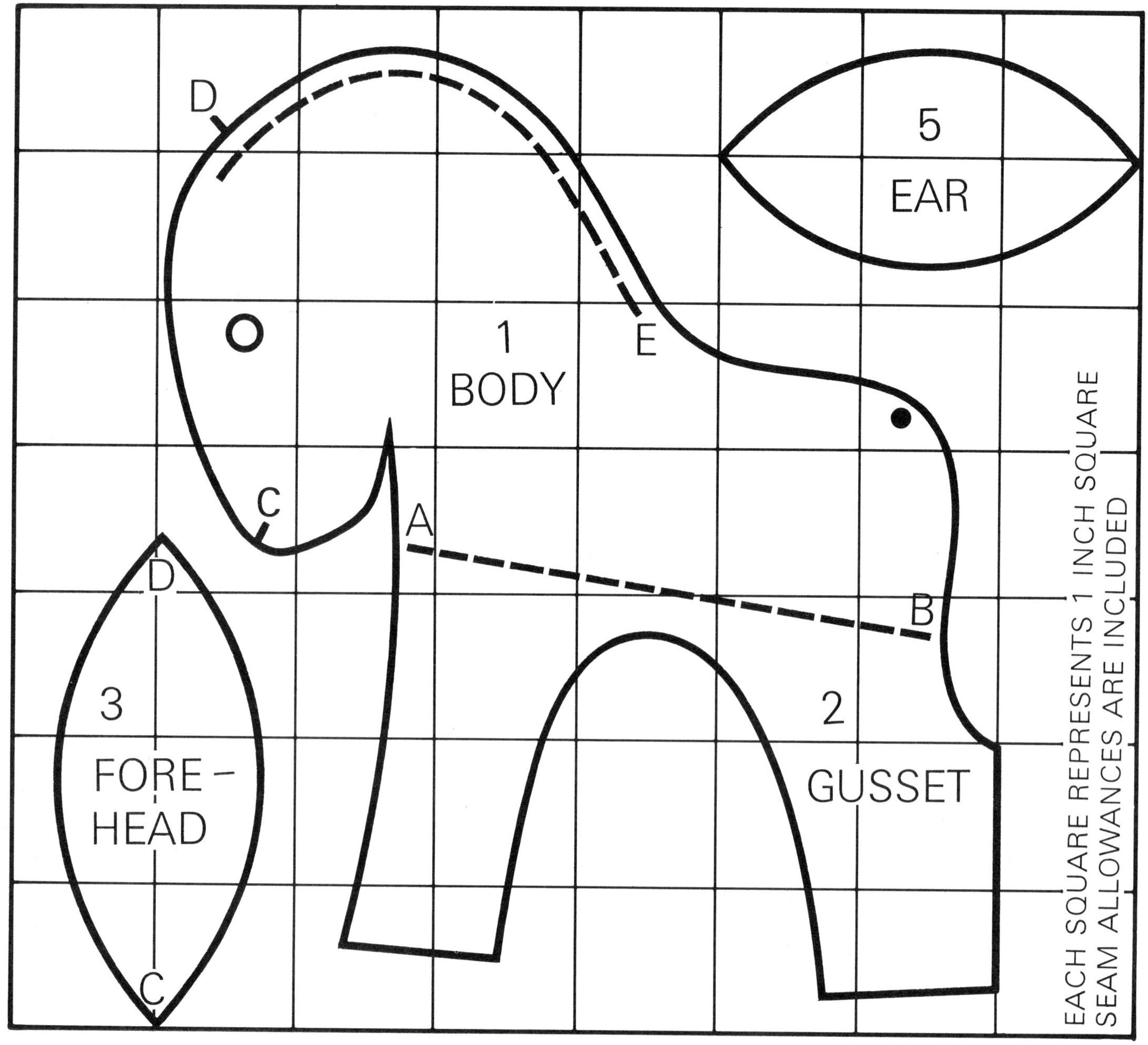